LORD OF THE TEMPLE

ERNST LOHMEYER

LORD
OF THE TEMPLE

A STUDY OF THE RELATION
BETWEEN CULT AND GOSPEL

Translated by
STEWART TODD

JOHN KNOX PRESS
RICHMOND, VIRGINIA

UNITY SCHOOL LIBRARY
Unity Village
Lee's Summit, Missouri 64063

Published in Great Britain by Oliver & Boyd Ltd., Edinburgh
and London, and in the United States of America by
John Knox Press, Richmond, Virginia

Library of Congress Catalog Card Number : 62-18409

A translation of *Kultus und Evangelium* by Ernst Lohmeyer,
published in 1942 by Kommissionsverlag Vandenhoeck &
Ruprecht, Göttingen

The Scripture quotations in this book are from the Revised
Standard Version of the Bible, copyrighted 1946 and 1952
by the Division of Christian Education, National Council of
the Churches of Christ in the U.S.A., and used by permission

ENGLISH EDITION

First published 1961

Translation © Oliver & Boyd Ltd

Printed in Great Britain

BS
2370
L 832 l
c. 1

To my friend
Anton Friedrichsen

FOREWORD

In the winter of the year 1939 I was invited by the Theological Faculty of Uppsala to give a series of lectures there. I was on active service in Poland when the invitation reached me but in spite of all the difficulties I was able, thanks to the helpfulness of the academic, military, and diplomatic authorities, to accept the invitation, and to deliver the lectures in Uppsala and again in Lund.

Since I had had very little time for preparation the lectures were delivered more or less extempore from notes, but as repeated requests came from Sweden that I should publish them it became clear that I should have to write them out in my brief spells of leave. I knew that the basic ideas must remain substantially the same but many things would be changed in detail. Whereas in a lecture it was sufficient to develop a meaningful line of thought, in a book it would be necessary to provide also the exegetical foundation of the line of thought. Wartime and unbroken military service did not permit me, however, to enter upon a detailed and learned discussion of every point made and to furnish all the proofs and examples. I decided therefore to pursue a middle course between the freedom of the lecture method and the more exacting discipline of the alternative. The informed and kindly reader will easily supplement what is missing. I have not written for the unkindly reader. Two important exegeses, that on Mk. XI. 15-17 and that on Mk.XII.1-12, have been reproduced at greater length in *Theologische Blätter*, 1941, Nos. 10 and 11, and also in *Zeitschrift für systematische Theologie*, 1941. The choice of the theme arose out of certain observations I made in my book *Galiläa und Jerusalem* and in my essays on the early Christian "Lord's Supper" and on the Johannine foot-washing. The essential connexion between this work and those others will be clear in the following pages. Nevertheless it is perhaps worth pointing out that the argument in these chapters is really quite independent of the argument in those others.

It would not have been difficult, had circumstances allowed it, to write a considerable volume on this great theme. I have had perforce to be content with a mere sketching of the bold outlines of the problem, and with such solution as our sources afford. I also decided to confine myself to what was to be gleaned, particularly concerning the history of Jesus, from the Synoptic Gospels. I am well aware that the other New Testament Scriptures should also have come within the scope of the study, especially the Johannine Scriptures, the Pauline Epistles, 1 Peter and the Epistle to the Hebrews. I believe also that seen in this context much new light would have been shed on these Scriptures, but it has not been possible to pursue these thoughts.

ERNST LOHMEYER

CONTENTS

PAGE

I. THE PROBLEM   I

The task, systematic or historical. Collapse of cult under the impact of the Gospel. The theme of the book. Concept of the cult. Cult as the action of God. Cult and community. Cult and history. Revelation—history. Cult in Judaism. Cult and the life of the nation. Cult—religion. The Temple. The priests. Holy birth, holy law, holy sacrifice. Cult as God's action in the present. Opposition between God and world, people and peoples. Cult and politics. Cult and ethics. Eschatological fulfilment. Cult prophecy. Cult and Pharisaism. Cult and Zealots. Cult and Anawim. Cult and apocalyptic.

II. THE CULT IN THE GOSPEL   24

Cultic tradition in Mark. Healing of one possessed of a demon (1.23-8). Healing of a leper (1.40-5). Healing of one sick of the palsy (11.1-12). A meal with tax-collectors (11.15-17). Saying about fasting (11.18-22). Sabbath observance (11.23-8). Clean and unclean (VII.1-23). Entry into the Temple (XI.1-11). Cleansing of the Temple (XI.15-17). Question of authority (XI.27-33). Parable of the vineyard (XII.1-12). Question of tribute (XII.13-17). The greatest commandment (XII.28-34). Apocalyptic discourse. Preparation for the Passover (XIV.12-17). Lord's Supper (XIV.18-25). Jesus' death. Cultic tradition in Matthew. In Luke. Approbation of the cult? Mt. v.23 f. (Sacrifice and brotherliness).

ix

III. THE GOSPEL ON CULT   62

The question. Kingdom of God=God's house,
Kingdom of God and Temple. Community. The
community of the rejected. Alternative to holy birth.
On the holy law. On sacrifice. Acts of healing.
Disciples. Customs concerning meals. The Last
Supper. The Bringer of eschatological fulfilment.
Jesus as teacher. As Son of Man. Jesus' death.

IV. CULT AND GOSPEL   92

Baptism and Baptist. Baptism and sacrifice. Galilee
in the history of Jesus. Jerusalem. Cult and
eschatology. Overthrow of the cult by the word of
the gospel. Faith. Works. Community. Meal.
Foundation of the new cult. The One who fulfils.
The Son of Man. His death. The original
community.

I. THE PROBLEM

THE sub-title of this book, the relationship between Cult and Gospel, covers an area of study which so abounds in questions and answers that it may appear almost presumptuous to hope to offer even a survey of the subject in these few lectures. One can attempt a basic understanding of the theme, one can consider the place which the two things, cult and Gospel, occupy within the Christian faith as a whole, and their mutual relationships to the faith; but in so doing immediately one encounters the much deeper questions why the proclamation of the Gospel requires the cult of a Christian Church and how this cult can make use of that Gospel. These in turn lead to further questions about the relationship between divine revelation and historical community, between God's word and man's response, God's *actio* and his people's *re-actio*; but then clearly we are at the heart of the Christian faith and in the thick of its deepest problems. Or else one can attempt a historical investigation of the subject and seek to determine how the Christian Church solved these basic problems at different periods of their historical development; but then we are confronted with a whole series of images which show us how the fundamental Gospel is reflected with constant novelty and variation and yet with a strange consistency in forms of worship, now moving onward with the majesty of a mighty river as in the days of great medieval cathedrals, now collecting itself so to speak in the inmost recesses of a quiet heart as in the publican's prayer. In one place the Christian cult is the transparent veil through which the original form of the Gospel glimmers pure and undistorted, in another it is the richly gathered garment in which the Gospel is almost hidden from view.

The task which is set us does not compass the almost unsurveyable span of Christian centuries, however, but is confined to the comparatively brief period of Jesus' own preaching mission and the early Christian transmission of it. Likewise we

I

do not intend to pursue all the ramifications of the basic problems, but to examine only the historical basis and origin of the problem. We shall be concerned with the beginning, with the ἀρχή, the first principle, which determined the course of development of the historical forms and the particularly Christian character of the cultic questions. The importance of this beginning, and the extent to which it also exceeds the narrower compass of theological and ecclesiastical questions, is easily gauged by having regard to a well-known historical fact. Everywhere in the time of Jesus, temples and altars raised their piles heavenwards; bulls, lambs, and doves were sacrificed, and priests discharged the bloody, holy duties of their office. As Paul went through the streets of Athens he saw in the streets and market-places altars dedicated to the wildest assortment of gods.

In the land of the Jews the one and only true Temple of God stood on holy Mount Zion. There almost constantly the smoke of sacrifices curled towards the skies; there untold throngs of priests and high priests, Levites and singers—the number has been estimated at a quarter of the whole population—lived by the holy service which went on daily, almost hourly, to the glory of the one God of heaven and earth. And yet before a hundred years had passed Pliny was lamenting the desolation of the temples and the abandonment of the sacrifices; the sanctuary in Jerusalem was burned to the ground and the Jewish people never again sought to offer to God a holy sacrifice in a holy temple. Since that time, wherever the Christian Gospel has taken root in heart and home, in palace and cottage, temple and sacrifice have disappeared from the land and the life of the peoples. There has never been anywhere any kind of counter movement, such as frequently follows revolutions of this radical nature, never any attempt anywhere to resuscitate the past, revitalise the old ways or reform them. Attacks on temples by the early Church and throwing down of altars are almost unknown. The sacrifices simply go out like a fire that is not tended, the temples fall, the altars disappear.

One is tempted to see in such revolutionary occurrences merely that kind of historical change where the old collapses and the new rises from the ruins. But it seldom happens that the collapse of the old comes with such inexorable finality, seldom is it so completely and profoundly based on thought and belief, and marked by such an utter renunciation of all force and violence, and seldom has a change of heart produced something so radically new as here. We are dealing here not merely with an obvious change in historical phenomena; we are dealing, to put it in a general way, with the appearance of new forces and the emergence of entirely new forms. They may clothe themselves, these new forces and forms, in familiar garments and make use of familiar media; yet they have an unmistakably new meaning, they wear a hitherto unknown air. The priest of the early Church does indeed borrow his vestments from the Jewish priesthood; sacrifice comes to life again, though somewhat later, changed into Mass and Eucharist, and several features of the ancient Temple—e.g. the altar—still continue to reappear in the Christian Church. Yet it cannot but be obvious that the old is really gone and quite literally all is become new.

When we ask about the ultimate causes of such a revolution we are confronting the real question involved in this study: what attitude was adopted in the gospel of Jesus to the problem posed by the cult and to the cult itself? The question is not to be side-tracked by the suggestion that the annihilation of the ancient cult by Christianity is connected with the old antagonism, taken over by Christianity, of Judaism versus heathendom. For, however sharply Judaism itself attacked all "heathenish" religions, it never attacked them merely on cultic grounds—that is true especially and yet also only to a certain extent of the Samaritans, who claimed to be the true guardians of the Law. Judaism merely set its own cult over against all other ancient forms of cult. Early Christianity, however, abandoned both the Jewish Temple and the Jewish cult; Jesus prophesied its early downfall, and drove money-changers and hucksters out of the sanctuary. In these facts there is a clear indication of something rather difficult to understand—a "No" to everything that is Jewish cult and at the same time a "Yes" which preserves the traditional elements that lie within it. From this enigmatic origin something too new and living to be changed came into being, the Christian cult, displaying itself first and foremost in Baptism and Lord's Supper, and holding sway triumphantly and permanently throughout the centuries of the Christian era.

In all the host of questions which these facts throw up, the one which concerns us is not merely how Jesus or the early community viewed the Jewish cult, or how they produced an early Christian cult. Our theme sets alongside the one "thing," the cult, the other "thing," the Gospel. The word Gospel is to be understood concretely with the only meaning it has in the Gospels themselves—the word and the event, both intimately bound up with the person of Jesus Christ. We are not therefore speaking here about any kind of outside influences and occurrences which might have brought about the change of cult indicated. Nor are we saying that the Jewish cult was brought to an end by the destruction of Jerusalem, nor that the Gospel extended beyond the bounds of its place of origin, attacking the worship of ancient gods and being engaged by them. These things do not determine or answer the question of the passing of all ancient cult and the emergence of Christian cult. One thing alone explains it, and that is the original content and the original self-sufficient power of the Gospel itself. The question of cult therefore is to be viewed in the light of this Gospel; it becomes the standard which makes a really and historically "new" worship necessary, it indeed becomes itself the only power that will create and fulfil its forms. Now of course all this makes the problem even more difficult, as is easily demonstrated; for where in the Gospel tradition do we find any words which could be taken to indicate the birth of a new cult? We look for them in vain in the Sermon on the Mount or in Jesus' parables. And if a story like that of the Cleansing of the Temple be quoted, so great and so eloquent is the silence that it seems none can regard it as having "merely" a historical (*historische*) significance. Nevertheless it would be fascinating to inquire for a little into the difference between what is "merely historical" (*historisch*) and what is not "merely historical" (*historisch*) and one then would reach, certainly after a careful examination of the merely historical, a proper and specifically dogmatic evaluation of history (*geschichte*).

The problem of cult therefore constrains us to go to the Gospel; not that we shall find in it all the answers writ large, but because we must seek out cultic references therein which have not been observed or else little heeded. Once alerted by some obviously cultic words and narratives, we shall go on to find countless more indirect pieces of evidence of the wealth of material that lies hidden not only in the cult itself but even more in the Gospel. Just as a familiar monument suddenly becomes new and alive when one views it from a different angle, so also the inexhaustible historical and objective wealth of the Gospel appears in a new light when we consider it with the cult, both as an idea and as a reality, constantly before us. It will also be necessary, therefore, to be clear about this idea and this reality of the Jewish cult since they constitute the pre-supposition of Jesus' attitude, and to that task we now address ourselves.

We German Protestants are rather inclined, perhaps misled by certain misunderstood words of Luther's, to regard cult as something subsidiary, something less vital than the divine power of revelation in the Word and the faith of a pure heart. But the briefest glance at the New Testament teaches us that the cult in a strict sense embraces the whole of revelation and of faith. When we read there that in God's world to come everything that goes on here will cease except the service and the praise of God; when again and again prayers and exhortation, psalms and confessions issue in the cry: "To the glory of God the Father"; when Paul professes it as the aim and the end of his work, "so that many will give thanks on our behalf for the blessing granted us" (II Cor. 1.11)—when we read these things it becomes immediately clear that the service of God is one of those immovable and apparently essential and fundamental things which will always be as they always have been. And if we look at the history of other religions, we find the idea of cult in all places and in the most varied forms, in the narrow compass of a simple saintly heart, in a great community of faith encompassing a whole nation, in outward gestures, in spoken confession, or in lonely contemplation. And yet cult and faith are not just synonymous. There is a sharp distinction: faith makes heart and world, time and space, one before God. Cult on the other hand is that God-directed activity which is based on a revelation regulated by holy rules and pursued by a society which is an historically existing entity and is rooted in such revelation.

Each of these attributes is important and significant. The beginning of all cult is an act of God; in the Old Testament one thinks of the election of the Patriarchs or the Covenant at Sinai. All cultic activity on the part of man is merely *re-actio* to God's *actio*, the response (*Antwort*) to His preceding word (*Wort*). This activity is, however, never the response of an individual, not even of a prophet or mystagogue; it is the response of a community, whether this community speaks directly as in the above-mentioned portrayals of the eschatological consummation, or expresses itself through individuals such as priests. Cult therefore implies community just as community implies cult, since both are based on God's revelation in history. Cult is only possible in community, community is only possible through cult; the more completely the community recalls and relates itself to the act of God that is the basis of its cult and fellowship, the greater is the power and grace of that cult. The more consistently cult clings to its own secret and guards it as God's wonderful act in the course of the years and the centuries, the more closely it binds the community together. It will be remembered, for example, how all turning-points in the history of Israel and of Judaism are related in this way to the cult: the people is really founded by the granting of the Covenant at Sinai, and it is then that the tabernacle appears; the kingship is inaugurated with the building of the Temple at Jerusalem; the Deuteronomic reform is a reform of the cult; after the Exile the new Jewish people is constituted with the rebuilding of the walls and the Temple, and collapses again with their collapse.

We may say that cult and community belong together as the individual and his activity in time belong together; then we are in fact saying that the temporal locus of the cult is in a real sense history and tradition. That act of divine revelation which once founded the cult and the community is historical event, to which heaven and earth, God and people together turn their gaze. As revelation it brings with it all the grace and all the demands, all the power and all the holiness of an act of God; as event it has all the reality of a human historical happening. Whether one lauds this act as miracle, therefore, or timidly reverences it as mystery, always it is the mid-point where God and people are bound together, or perhaps rather the binding medium of this connexion. For that reason again it is not simply a great event of the past, in the light of which or in the shadow of which the present lives, an event which loses its force as time passes. On the contrary, whenever in a later present one seeks the way to God then that event is contemporary or, to put it more accurately, that act which created cult and community is the present power which then and thereafter prepares the way to God, and the divine-human force which ensures the stability of the people in the present and in the future. In so far as it links up past and present and future in this way, or in other words in its canonical holiness, the cult is for the community the light which lights their way through time, the key to the enigmas of their passage, and their comfort through all the confusions of their history. Nearly all the great prophets of the Old Testament, Ezekiel, Deutero-Isaiah, etc., have portrayed the solution of all the historical enigmas of God's people in cultic images: "Then everyone that survives of all the nations that have come against Jerusalem shall go up year after year to worship the King, the Lord of hosts, and to keep the feast of booths" (Zech. xiv.16). Thus through the preservation and confirmation of the cultic ordinances the history of the people, even in times of need and disorder, is changed into the transparent web of God's acts, and the certainty of a glorious triumphant future is established.

However, within the history of the community there flows like a separate current a history which the cult, or more exactly the act of God which occasions the cult, itself directly produces. For this act has all the limited and conditioned characteristics of a single passing event and yet is of the nature of a holy revelation. The holy has therefore assumed the dimensions of time and place, and likewise time and place, land and people have become holy. This act and the institutions based upon it are valid for the whole people, but they are not made valid through the whole people. They permeate its history and are not consumed in it, they exist as a whole, as something inviolable, and for that very reason they are distinct from everything in history that is provisional—history being the

B

place of things defective and unfulfilled; they preserve their distinction even though the history of the community is not simply a history of the holy within it, but also of men within it. There is produced a lasting tension and an ever new reconciliation, not merely with the historically given conditions of the people or of the community but also within the sphere of the cult itself, since it is act and arrangement of men and at the same time act and arrangement of God; and the measure of this tension and reconciliation is the opposition and fellowship between God and the community or between God and the world. From the magnitude of this distinction there arises the inexhaustible wealth of forms and forces, each of them expressing again in miniature that mysterious unity and contrariety between all-embracing divine revelation and limited human event, each of them transitory like all human action and yet surviving for centuries and remaining as a living sign of God. From this holy distinction emerge sacrifice and rite, the priestly function and the priestly class, holy places and seasons, usages and buildings, to mention only a few—in short that tremendous wealth of sacred tradition which runs through the history of all peoples and religions. The extent and nature of this distinction vary very much, but the holy distinctiveness in itself or the distinctive holiness is everywhere an indestructible characteristic. It is the medium of that act of revelation which makes God an effective reality upon the earth, and it is at the same time a thing of the earth; it is both since this revelation has its appropriate place not in a transitory event but in eternity. In this way the sacred becomes history and history becomes sanctified, yet in both a fulfilment is required which is not history.

One might well ask whether this basic significance of the cult was appreciated by Jews in Jesus' time, and a chorus of voices would seem to say "no." When Temple and cult at Jerusalem had disappeared in the catastrophe of the year A.D. 70, a Jewish seer lamented and consoled his people in the words, "We have nothing save the Almighty and His law" (Syr. Bar. Apoc. 85.2). It was consolation in that the law was and became increasingly the one firm support of the outward life of the people, and the thing that really determined all thought and action. It was also lamentation in that the cult,

the real and living source of the holiness of God, was fouled
and lost under the ruins of city and Temple. The complaints
of later rabbis show clearly what this meant to the Jewish
people: "Since the day the sanctuary was destroyed an 'iron
curtain' has separated Israel and Israel's Father in heaven"
(Berach, 32b). Prayers' doors are closed, only tears' doors
remain open: "alas for all our deeds of expiation!" Likewise
in the Prayer of Eighteen Supplications the seventh runs:

> Bring again sacrifice
> To the holy place of Thy house,
> And receive Israel's burnt offering
> And her prayer in love and approbation.

On all festive occasions one was to remember with sorrow
the destruction of the Temple. If a man whitewashed his house
he should leave a part unwhitened in memory of Jerusalem.
One gathers from these reminders and these customs that in a
strange and immutable way, to base one's life only upon the
Law left one in need, even if it had also become in the course
of the centuries a saving necessity. The people is compelled to
live on with an open wound in its heart and without a Holy
Grail. For as a later writer puts it: "the world is founded
upon three things—the world, not merely the people or its
religion is so founded—on the law, on atonement, and on
the service of the priest." What does a statement like that
really mean in detail?

When Ezra and Nehemiah began to reassemble the Jewish
people in the Holy Land, they related their fortune to the
erection of the holy city and the holy temple; and when this
same people under political and syncretistic influences was in
danger of losing its pure priestly office, the Maccabaean
struggle broke out. Even in a quite superficial sense, therefore,
the existence of the people depended upon this pure operation
of the traditional cult; and, leaving out of account for the
moment the overlordship of the Romans, its polity did in fact
clearly reflect this. Priests possess outward power and moral
and spiritual leadership in all matters relating to the life of the
people. They are politicians, judges responsible for the
preservation of the good order of the state; they are also
advisers and pastors, teachers and scholars; and they are all

of these things, simply because they have charge of the sacred worship of the house of God.   But more important than these external features, which come down to us from the history of Jesus and of the early Christian community, is the theological significance of the cult.   In the time of Jesus it is more than just an historical inheritance from a glorious past, more than just the sign preserved through all difficulties of outward national and religious unity; it is the God-given way and means of bringing salvation to His people and His world.   In such a statement many questions are raised and as many answers given.

We have become accustomed to think of the faith of the Jewish people in the time of Jesus as essentially the religion of the Law; but one could with equal accuracy and error call it the religion of the cult, for the cult is a divine revelation just as much as the Law is.   Both were given to the fathers by God in a holy antiquity.   In the present the Law is declared only by reference to tradition and interpretation, but the cult attests itself daily—almost hourly—by its revelatory and sanctifying power wherever the smoke of divinely ordained sacrifice ascends to heaven.   The Law, especially in the Pharisaic and Rabbinic view, gives the individual his aim and mission in life; the cult gives the community the divine ground of its existence and its actual holiness, while to the individual it gives the possibility and the necessity of serving God and making atonement.   The Law is the expression of God's truth and norm, the cult is the expression of God's present reality and power.   God founded the people and bound Himself to it and through the people to each individual in it; the cult is therefore the basis of life, the Law is the imperative derived from it.   This sacred reality and validity of the cult is made clear in several ways.   In the Temple at Jerusalem there dwells His "Name," commanding reverence and showering blessing; the Temple is the source and site of all "glory" and sanctity.   One can tell from the story of Isaiah's vision in the Temple, one can tell from the fiftieth chapter of the Book of Ecclesiasticus (for all that it does also celebrate the Law as the light of all wisdom and godliness), just how much awe and reverence the spatial proximity of God in the Temple inspires, and how deeply the sacred office of the priest impresses the people as a divine event in a particular time and place. God is bound to this place because He has chosen to bind Himself to it. This fact, at once mystery and miracle, is the solution of all other mysteries and the essence of all miracles. Because this is "the holy habitation of the Most High" (Ps. XLVI.4) the priests themselves handle divine things and do divine works. This basic idea has also naturally been worked out more abstractly: the sanctuary at Jerusalem is an image of the heavenly "tabernacle," the service of the priests a likeness of the heavenly worship. It really does become true, therefore, in terms of this glorious reflexion, that people and priest do live and move and have their being in and with God. This idea is firmly established ever since the time of the prophet Ezekiel, who preached the "new" Temple, and became inviolable with Ezra and Nehemiah, who rebuilt the Temple when, inspired by eschatological hope, they sought to settle the people again in their native land. Land and people, priests and lay, become through this holy place God's peculiar possession, His earthly treasure. Why should only this people and land out of all the peoples of the earth have been selected to be the holy children and servants of God, one may ask. Here again is the answer: "I the Lord of heaven and earth, have chosen you and guided you from the beginning of creation that my sanctuary should be built among you for all eternity. And the Lord shall appear and all eyes shall behold him, and all shall know that I am the God of Israel and the father of all the children of Jacob and king upon mount Zion for ever; and Zion and Jerusalem shall be holy" (Jub. 1.28 ff.).

And when cult and Temple are so much a part of the life of the Jewish people and vice versa, it is inevitable that the man who bears responsibility for both, the priest, should gain for himself a certain air of sanctity. In the enthusiastic utterances of the writer of the Book of Ecclesiasticus one can feel his grateful and reverent pride in the High Priest (L. 5-7).

> How glorious he was when the people gathered round him
>   as he came out of the inner sanctuary!
> Like the morning star among the clouds,
>   Like the moon when it is full;
> Like the sun shining upon the temple of the Most High,
>   and like the rainbow gleaming in glorious clouds;
> Like roses in the days of the first fruits.

The priests are separated from the people (and yet also identi-
fied with the people) as the select group amongst them who
discharge the duties of the priestly office and the service of God,
just as in the Temple at Jerusalem the court of the priests is
separated off from those of the men and women and yet is
part with them of the same great sanctuary.   The priests guide
and defend the fortunes of the nation, reserve its internal
struggles, regulate all its affairs, indicate to the individual
the end and the manner of all his actions; and they are sanctified and empowered to do all this not because of any human
ordinance but because they are—the High Priest is often so
called—the earthly representatives of God.   Even when in
Jesus' time certain innovations tended to modify their function
—e.g. a greater number of lay representatives was permitted
in the Sanhedrin—even then there was no relaxation of cultic
obligations and the basic position of the priest remained
unaltered.   One of the fiercest feuds between Pharisees and
Sadducees concerned what to us would appear a negligible
question of cultic ceremonial detail.   And nowhere is the basic
and actual sanctity of the priesthood more clearly expressed
than in the eschatological hope that the day will dawn when
the whole people will be what now the priests are, a holy
people, a nation of priests: "ye shall be to me a kingdom of
priests and a holy nation" (Ex. xix.6).

For both priest and people, therefore, there arises the
question how this sanctity, which is as much a duty imposed
on men as it is a gift from God, is to be preserved; and for both
the answer is basically the same—sacred birth, sacred action,
and sanctifying sacrifice.   The priest is qualified for his sacred
work in virtue of his belonging to a particular family which is
or ought to be faultlessly pure, in virtue of a special diet and
special vestments which keep him from all impurity, and in
virtue of his ordering all his actions according to the rules
which have been given to him by God in holy revelation.   The
same kind of thing in a lesser degree is to be said about the
people: they are the seed of Abraham, children of the patriarchs (and it is well known how strenuously opposed the
Sadducees were to all foreign missions in marked contrast to
the Pharisees who would "traverse sea and land to make a
single proselyte" (Mt. xxiii.15)); they rely completely on the

Law which prescribes the manner and the aim of life, even in food and in dress, and differentiates them from all other peoples. But here again birth and the Law are only the two necessary presuppositions of a third, holy sacrifice. This sacrifice, whatever form it takes, serves a twofold end which in the last instance is one end, fellowship between God and nation and thereby fellowship within the nation. Sacrifice takes them back to the basic holiness of God and His heavenly host—a Rabbinic text says: "on the day of atonement the children of Israel shall be pure as the angels"—and makes God's sanctifying power and reconciling grace visible and effective in time. The cult is the means of mediation instituted by God between God and the nation or—as is sometimes quite logically stated—between God and the world. The cult is the one place where pure and holy things are effected on earth, for God permits "his name to dwell in the sanctuary," purifying, blessing, sanctifying, atoning, that the people so strengthened may always be able to make a fresh start on their way through an unholy and distracted world.

Birth, Law, and sacrifice are the three elements which sustain and constitute the priestly cult. How often do we find the Rabbis boasting: "ye are of noble birth," or: "I am a queen, the daughter of queens, beloved the daughter of beloved ones, holy the daughter of holy ones, pure the daughter of pure ones" (Mech. Exod. xv.2f., 44*b*). The divine-human nature of sacrifice, which in the course of time remains ever new and ever old, demands such pride in religious nobility of birth, since only so, only in virtue of what the individual quite fortuitously is, not in virtue of what he does or can do, does the ancient heritage from the patriarchs become valid and effective for children and children's children. Purity of sacrifice requires purity of birth in priest and in people, a purity which again is not a matter of human desert but of divine grace. It is in this sense that the boast is to be understood which says that at the Feast of Atonement the people become pure and holy "like newborn babes." The kind of holiness which birth gives to the individual or to the people is only a beginning, however, only a foundation; it has to be worked out in life and in history. And next to birth comes holy law, not pure works, again not human act, but divine revelation. Here again we see the prevailing tendency to connect the realisation of holiness solely with the action of God. There arises a difficulty here, however. The Law points the way to holiness but it does not give any holiness; it is fulfilled only in human behaviour, and therefore alongside God's demand for purity and holiness there is always the possibility of sin and error. In view of this gap between divine demand and human behaviour—a gap which does not exist when one is thinking of the holiness of God, but which is always present when one is thinking of human action and divine norm, the Law is not the real foundation of Jewish faith: beyond it there is that revelation by which God himself closes the gap—holy sacrifice. Thus the Law from this point of view becomes the God-given means of leading the people to the point where a holy sacrifice is offered and a sacred fellowship can be established. In other words one takes part in the cult not because it is commanded in the Torah; rather one fulfils the Torah in order to be pure enough to be able to take part in the cult. Similarly in the matter of pride of birth, it is not birth alone which makes the child a holy member of the people, but the cultic act of circumcision which brings it into the fellowship of the children of God. Just as a tree lets down its roots and seeks nourishment from the good earth in order to be able to lift its stem and its head to receive the twin blessings of light and air, so both individual and people need the twin bases, their lineage and their Law, in order to be able to receive from above the blessing of holy sacrifice and the fellowship with God guaranteed and instituted thereby. The cult is a crown and climax, with the holy shining beam of the Highest upon it, and the people come to dwell in its kindly shadow.

Where sacrifice, Law, and birth are thus understood to be united to produce the three-in-one miracle and sign of a God-given existence, there are of course several possible ways of interpreting its holiness in terms of life and history. Frequently the cult is extolled as the one true place where God deals with His own. "Hail ye Israelites!" cries Rabbi Akiba in the Atonement Day sacrifice; "By whom are ye purified and who cleansed you? Even your Father in Heaven!" (Joma VIII.9). In dealing with them He acts for their good, but does He act for their good *alone*? In Jesus' day there was considerable controversy about the scope of the cult, whether it was intended only for the nation or for the world as well. It is claimed on the one hand that the continuance of the world depends upon the Abodah (Pirke Aboth 1.2). On the other hand one finds statements like this: "God purifies Israel; and if one says also another nation . . . nevertheless know . . . Israel alone he forgives" (Pesiq. R.45, 185b). The question at issue was never resolved. Both views, the narrow particularist and the wider, so-called universalist view, remain irreconcilably opposed. But both have this in common, that in them God is recognised as the only source and His nation as the only recipient of grace. This has another important consequence; the more the cult is regarded and trusted as the one source of all sanctification, the more deeply all human action retires into the shadows of unholiness. God and world stand over against one another like darkness and light, above and below; and even if in such distinction they are nevertheless connected to one another by invisible bands, it is God alone who has the power to "make peace" between the opposites. Thus the opposition holy-unholy, heavenly-earthly based on the cult produces in time the palpable elements of an apocalyptic expectation of an End, in which by the act of God alone peace takes the place of conflict and holiness of unholiness.

The same circumstances which produce this fundamental opposition and the apocalyptic solution of it give rise to one further possibility, however, which appears to be completely at variance with the first. If the cult represents the inconceivable unity of divine and human action, it necessarily exalts to a position of peculiar importance this historical people and its priesthood, to which God's sanctifying service is entrusted. Although this nation treads its dark and insignificant way in paths of good or evil, of error or faithfulness, nevertheless as the agent of the metaphysical, which creates blessedness and holiness within history, it becomes the chosen, holy people of God, the royal priesthood and whatever other title the Old Testament bestows. One does not ask how it is possible that a nation becomes the holy people of God: it is just a fact, it has been so arranged by God, and it is constantly renewed in the priests' service. There is a holy land, a holy city, a holy house in which God makes "his name to dwell"; and this land and people is year by year made clean of every spot in the great feast and sacrifice of Atonement, so that they are pure like the angels in heaven. Then, however, it comes to be regarded as part of this nation's history that they are elevated above all the peoples. The latter become unholy "nations" and this one nation, which alone God sanctifies, becomes their lord. If this lordship has not yet been attained in history, it will come; for this is basic law authenticated by God himself, that the course and content of this nation's intimate relations with God should be reflected in the course and content of their historical destiny and should finally be fulfilled in it. Cultic and political images are therefore constantly being employed together to describe the real present and the eschatological future. God—or His eschatological envoy—is king, He makes peace among the nations or annihilates them, that "we might serve him . . . in holiness and righteousness before him, all the days of our life" as the psalm of Zechariah (Lk. 1.75) quite simply puts it. What is here spoken of as a longed-for fulfilment easily commandeers even the present: the cult is a sanctifying power now and always, which is given to this nation as it wanders through the errors and confusions of life. There arises, therefore, the danger that the contemporarily historical assumes the proportions of the ever-holy, and the holy is debased to the level of the politically expedient. The priest becomes politician, the politician becomes priest. The Maccabeans are an obvious example, and the party of the Sadducees remains for centuries a living illustration of how constant a factor the mixing of cult and politics was. The Zealots did something rather different, they combined holiness and power. They did not, however, leave it to God to work out how the holy within the nation should become powerful and power become holy; they took the matter into their own hands as their task. They contended vigorously for the freedom of the nation because the holiness of the Temple was assured by God; and so unshakable was their faith and their contention that not even the flames of the burning Temple in the year A.D. 70 could daunt it. But however the bond between cult and politics was established in detail—and for both parties it was a necessary bond—and although the outworking of it often brought them into sharp opposition, nevertheless, despite their differences, they based their action on the belief that it was God who had entrusted the preservation of His "house" and the leadership of His people to them, and that God would carry these two undertakings through to a final and complete fulfilment, no matter what struggles might be encountered without or within.

The relationship of cult and politics is the one important feature of Jewish religion, at once to commend, because the sanctification of the world as well as the nation is involved, and to condemn, because every attempt to combine them is a mingling of the sacred with the profane. The second no less important feature is the relationship of cult and ethics. The cult lives and has its being in certain individual actions which, because of their origin in ancient revelation and because of their revered tradition, are separated off from all profanity and belong to a context of really valid sanctity. And when in Jesus' time we find the effort being made to bring every little act and trick such as hand-washing within this context by means of detailed regulations—a magnificent effort in its way to sanctify the profane—the question does seriously arise whether God's holy revelation can be expressed in a particular kind of outward action and behaviour. If it is revelation it demands the whole man and the whole people at all times— and only before God are individual and people a whole; it demands both in a way so comprehensive and complete that it disregards all historical particularity. There is therefore in all cultic considerations and in all cultic demands a secret tension between the particularity of outward cultic forms and the universality of its inward sacred reality; and all outward splendour of cultic action and all intensity of cultic sanctification serve only to cover up this tension, not to resolve it. This tension was recognised by the Jews, of course; they knew well that what was demanded of them, of the individual as well as of the nation, was not merely the fulfilment of cultic regulations but also the fulfilment of moral laws—in Jewish terminology what was demanded was the fulfilment of the entire Torah. The Torah did in fact contain in its amazing richness both things, both regulations which shared this particularity of the cultic sphere and obligations which shared the universality of ethics. Alongside the commandment: "thou shalt love thy neighbour" stands another concerning the nature of the sacrificial animal and the method of sacrifice. But what is the significance of such a juxtaposition? Should the moral commandment supplement the cultic duty in order that complete and utter holiness may be achieved? Then in that case both are reduced to the status of something limited and incomplete. Should the moral commandment alone be recognised as binding, as the absoluteness of the demand suggests? Then the cultic action becomes a dumb, empty, meaningless show. If on the other hand the observation of cultic regulations is *the* religious obligation, then all moral demands become superfluous and of no account. There is no doubt that Judaism strove with all its might to resolve this tension which so endangered its very existence. It demanded both of its people, as the law commanded, one alongside the other, it could do no other. But the holiness for which God founded and towards which He directed all cult, was more than merely the sum of cultic purity and ethical innocence; it was certainly the constant and complete and only source of both, but that is a different matter. And therefore the mere adding together of cultic regulations and moral commandments must come to grief unless there were outside supports to hold it together. These outside supports were in this case ancient tradition, established custom, and something which embraces both, the common life and history of the nation itself.

The tension between cult and ethics can therefore be held and hardened, it cannot be resolved. The national context is too constricted; it is not the proper place at all for ideas either of cultic holiness or of pure morality.

There can be a resolution of the tension only where both things are one and the same thing, in other words where a real holiness coincides with the norm of the good and the latter fulfils itself in the former. The tension is resolved eternally in God alone. It will remain, therefore, as long as man and nations live in the light and darkness of the earth, it is as old as the world. Men and nations will not resolve it—how could that which is the basis and the aim of their existence be in their disposing? It will be resolved for them and with them when "heaven and earth shall pass away." With profound good sense, therefore, some sections of Judaism longed for a new Jerusalem and a new Temple which should come down to earth from heaven. The day of eschatological fulfilment is also the day of sanctification. Thus the problem of cult and ethics leads at a higher level to the same end to which the problem of cult and politics tended. In God's hand alone resides the power at the last day to sanctify the nation and the nations. And in this eschatological sanctification there is achieved for those things which in the world and in history are always separate in indissoluble unity, an identity; the particular of cultic holiness *is* the universal of the norm of moral good.

It will be remembered in this connexion that in the history of the Jewish people men repeatedly emerged who fought against the idea of the sole validity of cultic holiness and the sole imperative of cultic prescriptions; and it is proof of the greatness of that people that their prophets did so with such passion and with such inexorable perspicacity. From the time of the first literary prophets onwards a chorus of voices is heard sharply denouncing the ways of the cult and refusing to distinguish between the worship of God and helping one's neighbour: "I desire steadfast love and not sacrifice" (Hos. vi.6). Or one thinks of Ps. li.17:

> The sacrifice acceptable to God is a broken spirit;
> a broken and contrite heart, O God, thou wilt not despise.

Such quotations from the Prophets and the Psalms could be easily multiplied; moreover the reasons for such an outcry have been so frequently examined that it is unnecessary to speak of them here at any great length. They sound an unmistakable warning against a way of thinking which relies only on the divine origin of a national cult. Yet, however important these voices are for an understanding of Jesus' preaching—the Gospel of Matthew twice puts the word from Hosea in Jesus' mouth—and however much they have been hailed as alone having the ring of genuine Old Testament religion, the fact remains that they intensify the problem rather than solve it. They do indeed make the good deed the decisive standard, and the will of a righteous God the only norm of action, but thereby they only prepare the ground and provide the weapons for the battle to take place. One can gauge from the sorrow expressed over the destruction of Solomon's Temple, or from the glowing hope of a new sanctuary, how closely even for a Jeremiah or an Ezekiel the fact of the cult is linked up with the prophetic demand. No prophet of the Old Testament ever penetrated to the real root of the conflict between cult and ethics. For however bravely each of them proclaimed the true will of God—and that means essentially "for all peoples"—he remained in his threats and in his condemnations a prophet of his own people, a people built on the foundation of the permanence of the cult. However vehemently he demanded ethical righteousness instead of cultic purity he never rejected Temple and sacrifice altogether. A prophet like Third Isaiah makes a profound contribution therefore when, casting his gaze to the eschatological future, he sees the problem of the nation and the nations and the problem of cult and ethic solved in one and the same promise:

> And the foreigners . . .
> these will I bring to my holy mountain,
>   and make them joyful in my house of prayer;
> their burnt offerings and their sacrifices
>   will be accepted on my altar;
> for my house shall be called a house of prayer
>   for all peoples.
>
> (Is. LVI.7)

We shall see later how Jesus continued farther along the way here indicated, to the goal at which the community which He calls and which hears Him is itself the eschatological praying fellowship of the sanctified. But that too implies that in a national context the problem of cult and ethic is insoluble, and can only be solved where, above and beyond the nation and the nations, above and beyond all "particulars," divine or human, holy or unholy, there is founded the eschatological community.

In post-exilic times the more the prophetic word was recognised as holy, a development assisted by the bitter experience of the Babylonian captivity, the less chance there was of finding a solution to the problems of cult and ethics and cult and politics. One may perhaps also mention the Pharisaic movement here, especially if it stemmed from the circle of the Chasidim, as an attempt to shake off the autocracy of a cult which had become unholy and to build anew on a holier foundation. For when really for the sake of the holiness of Temple and priesthood they "separated themselves," they did in fact find in the careful examination and fulfilment of the Torah the principle which is at the root of all cultic ordinances and all cultic worship. Thus there appeared alongside the holiness which the cult knows, the righteousness which comes from observance of the Law; and time and again the commandments of the Torah comprised the cultic worship. Yet the Pharisees never impugned the cult itself. On the contrary in many cases they became the champions of the most strict cultic holiness. In such ceaseless effort the deeper problem of the relationship of cultic worship to morality remained unobserved and unsolved. The questions at issue figure largely in the thinking of two other groups which, though minority groups, have nevertheless become very important for the history of Jesus. These are the Zealots on the one hand and the Anawim on the other. We do not have a great deal of information about them and what we have is inexact, but we do know that in the political struggle of the Zealots against Roman overlordship the idea of the inviolable holiness of Temple and city, nation and land was uppermost. John of Gishala, we know, maintained his suicidal struggle against the Roman legions for four years in this cause, and even amidst the crumbling ruins of the city looked for deliverance by the appearance of a triumphant Messiah from and in the holy Temple. It is also well known that the Zealot party was particularly strong in Galilee; one of Jesus' twelve disciples belonged to it, and as a disciple still retained the at once distinctive and honourable surname "the Zealot." Here the cult has become the fixed and immovable basis of men's outlook, so holy that it demands life and blood from each individual and so concrete that what God has given and does give may and must be defended by force of arms if necessary. The Anawim represent the opposite extreme, and it was among them that Jesus grew up and found His most sympathetic audience. Their whole religious outlook can be termed an eschatological pietism; it based itself on the Law and put its trust in the Law's promises, it turned to the fathers and looked away beyond the darkness of the present to the near or distant light of an eschatological redemption. Opposed to all extravagant ideas of a Messianic glory the Anawim preserved within a limited sphere the true spirit of Old Testament prophecy and sought to work it out in terms of poverty and righteousness. Perforce or voluntarily, consciously or unconsciously, this pietism was really far removed from all cult; the salvation it desired belongs to the time of the fathers and will return at the end-time. The holy city and the holy house in it become then the eschatological gift of an eternal and undisturbed rest (II Esdras VIII.52), and the present Temple is as it is understood in Is. LVI.7, the house of prayer. The present life is concerned with the tradition and the saintliness of the fathers, that we should serve God "in holiness and righteousness all the days of our life" (Lk. 1.75). Here to all intents and purposes the moral side of religious life, the side opposed to cult, has usurped all significance and validity; and all rights and hopes normally connected, for the individual or for the nation, with sacrifice and with the Temple are relegated to God and to the time of eschatological fulfilment.

Perhaps also in certain prophetic apocalyptic ideas which form a remarkable foil for several of the sayings of Jesus there are traces of both the above-mentioned emphases. According to an ancient idea which we find in the Psalms and in the prophets, the holy Mount Zion with its city and Temple is the centre of the world, and Jerusalem is the mother of the peoples. Two quotations will suffice:

Thus says the Lord God: This is Jerusalem: I have set her in the centre of the nations, with countries round about her   (Ezek. v.5).

or

On the holy mount stands the city he founded;
    the Lord loves the gates of Zion
    more than all the dwelling places of Jacob . . .
And of Zion it shall be said, "This one and that one were born in her;
    For the Most High himself will establish her."
The Lord records as he registers the peoples,
    "This one was born there."
                              (Ps. LXXXVII.1-2, 5-6)

The city and house of God will therefore embrace all nations at the day of fulfilment. A later Rabbinic quotation runs:

The land of Israel lies in the centre of the world, Jerusalem lies in the centre of the land of Israel, the holy precincts lie in the centre of Jerusalem, the Temple lies in the centre of the holy precincts, the ark of the covenant lies in the centre of the Temple, the foundation stone lies before the ark of the covenant. For on it the world is founded.

(Midr. Tanchuma, ed. Choreb, p. 444.15-18)

There revolves around this place, therefore, the eschatological destiny, not merely of Israel but of all nations. "When God will come into his Temple then the world is renewed, when the living waters bubble over the foundation stone to spill on Zion, the whole world is cleansed; when wisdom has once made her dwelling in the Temple at Jerusalem the stream of wisdom will overflow and become a sea, compassing the whole earth." That is how B. Sundkler once expressed these ideas. Perhaps they represent the atmosphere in which Jesus lived more than the direction followed in His preaching; but how alive and significant the story of the Cleansing of the Temple becomes when one sees it in the light of this idea, what a wealth of background becomes available, say, for the saying about the chief and corner stone, and how directly from such an idea do these words appear to stem;

Come unto me all ye that labour and are heavy laden, and I will give you rest.

For the Temple is the house of God's rest (Is. LXVI.1; II Esdras VIII.52). But that is to anticipate later considerations.

The problems associated with the idea of the Jewish cult and with the cult as it actually was are unlimited and are of tremendous importance. That at least must have become clear by now. They press for solution not only within the context of the Jewish people and its faith, but wherever the message of a new faith is proclaimed. We are entitled to ask, therefore, as an objective and historical question, what answer the Gospel of Jesus can give to the problem of the cult; and though the answer may be but dimly perceptible in our documents that does not relieve us of the duty of inquiring.

C

II. THE CULT IN THE GOSPEL

ANY attempt to solve the problem of cult and Gospel in the history and in the preaching of Jesus must necessarily be preceded by careful examination and elucidation of the wealth of material bequeathed to us in the Gospel tradition, some of which is obvious, but even more of which lies hidden. We shall examine well-known words like priest, temple, sacrifice; cultic concepts such as forgiveness of sins and holiness; ritual stipulations such as those about purity and impurity; and ecclesiastical practices such as observance of the Sabbath and fasting. Even so we shall not obtain a unitary picture of Jesus' attitude and the gospel attitude but only so many inferences and indications of a living and original unity.

Examining the Gospel of Mark in the way indicated, we make at once a remarkable discovery. We find that considerable sections of the narrative contain no reference to cultic matters whatsoever, and that almost all the cultic material is confined to three related sections, sections which also have a marked connexion with particular districts in which Jesus worked. Is there perhaps some correspondence between cultic outlooks and geographical situation? The accounts of Jesus' first appearance in Capernaum and of the subsequent journey through Galilean territory are steeped in cultic conceptions and concerned with many specific cultic matters (1.20-III.6). At the point where Jesus crosses over into heathen districts there comes the great discourse about cleanness and defilement. And in His last days in Jerusalem it would seem that Temple and cult constitute the most important problems of all those posed by the entry of Jesus into the holy city and solved only by His death (XI.1-XV.40). Let us begin with the first group of narratives having cultic significance, the group connected with Galilee.

Right at the beginning of Jesus' public ministry Mark's Gospel reports the healing in the Synagogue at Capernaum of a man possessed of an unclean spirit. The sick man cries to the

24

Master: "I know who you are, the Holy One of God" (1.24).
How significant this nomenclature was for the early Christian
can be gauged from the fact that the Fourth Gospel makes it
the basis of the great confession made on behalf of the twelve
(vi.69). In Jewish religion the name has, of course, a very
long history and various usages. It is used of priests who
"serve" God on earth and angels who "serve" him in heaven.
Occasionally, however, it is applied to others, to a prophet
perhaps or a saintly person. Even the Jewish people itself is
sometimes called "the holy people of God." But it is clear
from our narrative that even when the use of the word is
extended cultic ideas predominate. It is "an unclean spirit"
that hails Jesus, and between the Holy One and the demon
there is the cultic distinction of clean and unclean. It is this
holiness which gives the Master the power to "destroy" the
demon. His work is therefore to exterminate the demonic
"uncleanness," first of all in this one sick man, but then also—
for the demon speaks of "us," meaning all demons which have
their unclean being within God's people—to exterminate the
demons in all other sick folk within this people. But to eradi-
cate uncleanness from the people is the essential function of the
High Priest, who is also called the Holy One of God, fulfilling
his work of sanctification particularly at the great Festival of
Atonement. Here are Master and High Priest with the same
name and about the same business. The juxtaposition serves
to emphasise the difference, however. The one is a work of
sanctification bound up with sacrifice and theory, daily and
yearly repeated. The other is a greater thing altogether,
effective by the mere word and presence of the Master and
really "destroying" the demon. The priest may be called
"Holy One of God": here is "*The* Holy One of God."

The conflict, not apparent until that incident, appears again
in another story of healing (Mk. 1.40-5) in Jesus' own words.
To the leper whom He has "made clean" of his disease Jesus
says: "show yourself to the priest, and offer for your cleansing
what Moses commanded, for a proof to the people." This
passage is frequently interpreted as meaning that Jesus was
recognising existing cultic requirements, or at least not questioning them. But the more correct exegesis is rather different,
for wherever the formula "for a proof unto them" occurs the

reference is to the proof over against an unbelieving, God-
forsaking world. Therefore here it is the priests who are the
unbelieving enemies of Him who performed this miracle, they
are enemies even before they see it; and the sacrifice offered by
the healed leper is to serve not merely to prove the "cleanness"
of the man but by means of this proof to bear witness to the
power of the agent of eschatological fulfilment, to whom in
reality the commandment of Moses refers.   The conflict
between Jesus' healing power and priestly sacrifice is thus made
abundantly clear; the sacrifice is to point to the means "which
Moses commanded," but at the same time to the end of sacrifice
and priesthood, and Jesus' work has the as yet veiled object of
"destroying sacrifice," to quote from an apocryphal saying.

   The word about forgiveness of sins in the story of the healing
of the man sick of the palsy goes even farther (Mk. 11.1-9). The
argument which "certain of the scribes" offer to support their
accusation of blasphemy, that only One can forgive sin, and
that One is God, would generally be accepted but the underlying implication might not.   The question Jesus' word of
forgiveness had raised was not whether or not another besides
God has the same power, but who has power from God or
through God to forgive sins. The Jewish answer is clear and
traditional: God forgives sins on the basis of the sacrifice
commanded by Him and through the priest commissioned by
Him. Jesus' word is: "the Son of Man has power." Here
then we have the cult once ordained by God, and the Son of
Man, now sent by God, ranged against one another in sharp
opposition. The claim of the cult is so exclusive that anyone
is considered a "blasphemer" who disputes it. On the other
hand the power which Jesus' word of forgiveness brings to bear
upon the sickness of the palsied sufferer cannot take its place
alongside cultic ordinances but must of necessity replace them.
What might have seemed a possible co-existence turns out to be
a deadly enmity. The "enemy" is in effect saying: "forgiveness is not through priest and sacrifice, but only through
the Son of Man." The story does not say this in so many words,
but it is only if this is implied that there is any meaning in the
question "whether is it easier . . .?" It has often been suggested that the writer is establishing here a connexion between
sin and illness as there is in the Old Testament, though Jesus

Himself definitely discredited such an idea once and for all (Lk. XIII). There is certainly a connexion, yet it is not between sin and sickness in the victim but between the power to forgive sin and to heal sickness which the Master possessed. Because the Son of Man is holy, "*The* Holy One of God," He brings salvation (σωτηρία in the full New Testament sense and in the sense of the Aramaic original): because the holiness of the Son of Man comprises both true cultic and moral purity and healing power, He both forgives sins and heals sickness. That is why Jesus can ask "whether is it easier . . .?" It would be meaningless if it served only to depreciate the power of the Son of Man; it is meaningful because by virtue of His holiness He possesses the double gift and the double task, forgiveness of sin and healing of sickness: there is consequently a double act involved. The healing is the palpable proof of God's intervention, witnessing now against sacrifice and priesthood and for the Son of Man. Even more significant, Jesus' words are uttered on His own authority. He does not submit the fact of the forgiveness of sins to divine judgment yet to be passed. He assumes that such a judgment is already given in the presence of the Son of Man, and is proved to dull obtuse man by the healing power of His word. The time has come when the sins of the people are finally blotted out, the Son of Man is there who forgives them—all the significance of the cult institutions pales before the at once hidden and revealed reality of this eschatological event. True they were once founded by God and sanctified, but now they become a mere work of man; their end comes ever nearer the more clearly this consummation becomes reality. In this opposition two different things are involved. The one is that it is the eschatological work of the Son of Man "to forgive sins," and all power of word and miracle serves as sign and foreshadowing of that great end. That is why in the Nativity story in Matthew's Gospel it is expressly stated "He . . . shall save his people from their sins." The other is that the historical work of Him who bears the name Son of Man is directed against the Temple and the cult, and the opposition is the more pronounced the more the as yet hidden and eschatological Son of Man is revealed and does reveal Himself. Where He remains hidden this opposition also remains hidden: where He reveals Himself

He also creates the rift. One of the most remarkable features of this story is the fact that it foreshadows this tremendous opposition and the eschatological tension involved, all under cover of a discussion.

The stories which follow confirm that we are not dealing here with an isolated incident and an isolated idea, but with the one basic and inexhaustible concept which determines and permeates all the others. In the accounts of the meal Jesus shared with publicans and of the controversy about fasting, it might seem difficult to distinguish cultic issues; and certainly the two questions raised were considered at the time rather from the point of view of nationalism or general ecclesiasticism. Nevertheless cultic motifs are also present; e.g. "tax-collectors and sinners"—sin always implies cult, and fasting is based on a cultic regulation however widely practised it may have been. Jesus' response and reactions in these situations are therefore very important.

The fact that the Master "eats and drinks with tax-collectors and publicans" meant, according to Jewish belief at that time, a deliberate offence against binding cultic commandments, according to which whoever associated with such people was considered to have made himself one of them, to be unclean, and to have excluded himself from the fellowship of the faithful. Jesus ignored these commandments. He broke the all-too-rigid ritual rules not, however, from any feeling of general religious licence but simply and quite straightforwardly, if shockingly, because He believed He was eating the eschatological meal with His own—that means precisely with the outlawed, the tax-collectors and sinners. This sovereign freedom from the customary cultic restriction was born of the profound and basic belief that "the kingdom of God is at hand," and the freedom was the greater the less Jesus emphasised it. He knew that there and then in the fleeting hour of a friendly meal shared with despised men and renegades was represented the eternal and fulfilled community of the "holy": therefore He set Himself against the cultic institution which outlawed these same "tax-collectors and sinners." Here again, obviously this is Jesus in terms of His eschatology questioning the holiness of ritual injunctions, and for confirmation there are the two uncultic but quite pointed sayings which are included in the story of the meal. I do not need to take time to establish the point that "calling sinners" is closely related to "forgiving sins." As above so here the opposition to the cult is clear. As it is the task of cultic institutions to expel sinners, so it is the privilege and task of the eschatological Son of Man to "call sinners."

The word about fasting is even more daring. Fasting was practised for several reasons, but a glance at the calendar of the Jewish religious year makes it perfectly clear that fasting was based on ideas of cultic purity and was designed for that end. A ten-days' fast preceded the Festival of Atonement, for example, and priests fasted before every service in the holy place. For "sons of the bridechamber," however, fasting, according to Jesus, is neither necessary nor possible any more. Life with the Master lifts them into a sphere which is above the everyday context of all former obligations, where questions of right and wrong, commandment or prohibition, vanish like smoke. The fullness and festiveness of the eschatological day, dawning with the presence of the "Bridegroom" among men, have overcome all cultic difficulties.

The problem posed by Jesus' attitude to the Sabbath is similarly solved. One sees only one aspect of the solution, however, if one interprets the narratives and sayings about the Sabbath as indicating that a morally good action should take precedence over the observance of the third commandment. As in all questions involving cult and ethics—we shall have to look more closely at this later—Jesus' acts of healing on the Sabbath are not adequately explained either in terms of good actions or of help in human need. These acts of healing are primarily signs of the breaking in of the time of eschatological fulfilment: "if it is by the finger of God that I cast out demons, then the kingdom of God has come upon you" (Lk. XI.20). These "signs" are accomplished in virtue of the power of the eschatological time of fulfilment and the breaking of the Sabbath which they involve is similarly explained. Eschatological fulfilment knows no limitations; it conflicts with all the restrictions which have emerged from the cult. "The Son of Man is lord of the Sabbath." Nor can one dispute this argument by making reference to the disciples. It is true the disciples also broke the Sabbath (Mk. II.23-8) but their reason for doing so was even less ethical; at most it was that they were hungry. Yet even if that were unequivocally the case it would hardly provide the ultimate motive. Present need and future fulfilment are so inextricably bound up together in the preaching of Jesus that wherever the one exists the other exists also. The disciples have freedom to pluck ears of corn on the Sabbath not only because of their actual need but also in virtue of the "wedding" hour which makes them "sons of the bridechamber." Yet another aspect of the question of breaking the Sabbath is adumbrated in Mk. II.27: "The Sabbath was made for man, not man for the Sabbath." This vindication of their action refers to God's original order at Creation; it is related in that respect to the order that has grown up according to a very similar Rabbinical saying. But this order from the first of times also corresponds exactly to that of the last times, so that here again we have a reappearance of eschatology. There is an obvious comparison between the divinely sanctified man of the approaching end and the divinely created man of the distant beginning. Mark makes no mention of a breaking of the Sabbath justified by the fact that it was in a good cause; Luke does, but we shall revert to that problem later.

Reviewing this group of narratives and looking forward to the next chapter, one is very forcibly struck by the fact that where Jesus has to do battle or face opposition there are cultic matters involved. Is the converse of that also true, that where cultic matters are involved it means strife for Jesus? In ensuing chapters there is a complete absence of feud and of all cultic interest; they take a more positive line in contrast to their earlier counterparts which are directed against Jesus' enemies. Only when He leaves Galilee and crosses into heathen territories again does the conflict break out and cultic questions reappear (ch. VII).

In the course of the great indictment of "Pharisees and Scribes from Jerusalem"—both parts of the designation are significant but especially the geographical, Jerusalem not Galilee—there occurs the well-known saying (Mt. XV.11 and Mk. VII.15) which is called a parable:

Not what goes into the mouth defiles a man; but what comes out of the mouth, this defiles a man.

What is involved here is in the strictest sense a cultic axiom. If it is the task of the cult to keep holiness holy in the world, then obviously there must be certain criteria preserving the distinction between holy and unholy, clean and unclean. Whoever seeks to interfere with these interferes therefore with the fundamentals of the cult and of the life of his nation. Jesus' word is a throwing down of the gauntlet in bitter fury. The fact that in both parts of the sentence the principal clause is the same and the one subordinate clause is the counterpart of the other is a clear indication of Jesus' anger and sarcasm. The content of the sentence is even clearer and even more important. The first half presupposes the opposite thesis: that "what goes into the mouth defiles a man"—a quite obvious generalisation based on specific ritual food restrictions and an equally obvious ironical twisting of them. The undisguised sarcasm of the parallel: "what goes into the mouth" and "what comes out of the mouth," is perhaps even more eloquent still—as if for "a man" food and word could mean the same. Because the champion of the challenged cultic rubric omits the one thing Jesus considers important, Jesus takes the opportunity to emphasise it by describing it in words which reverse cultic instructions but nevertheless resemble them. It is for that reason Scripture has called this saying of Jesus a parable (Mk. VII.17; Mt. xv.15); it actually disguises what is meant but in such a way that it really expresses it more clearly. At one fell swoop, therefore, all instructions and restrictions concerning food are cast aside in favour of the word "that proceedeth out of the mouth"; and there is not the slightest allusion to the fact that these instructions written in Holy Scripture are part of God's holy law for His holy people.

What is even more significant is the fact that in this word Jesus transfers the whole question of purity from the plane of material externals to that of man's inner self. Man is no longer confronted by a world of things holy and unholy, divine and devilish in frightening variety, reducing him to helpless servitude of a vague and inexhaustible imperative; rather there emerges in unmistakable superiority the inner world of the human heart which alone is able to make a man holy or unholy, clean or unclean. This is a second creation comparable to the creation of the world by God's word; that creation belonged to the time of the beginning, this creation belongs to the time of the end. Man is free in this world which is given him to be at his service or for his pleasure; the outer limits are obliterated, all barriers raised by ancient religions and peoples are broken down, and the context of the problem of holiness is no longer an infinite world but the inexhaustible possibilities of the heart of man. It does indeed look as if the second half of the saying was referring only to the word that comes out of man's mouth, but as is well known, word and thought in Aramaic are almost identical. This only dimly veils the basic and more profound truth that all experience is bound up with words or gives rise to words. Therefore the otherwise quite general expression "what comes out of the mouth" denotes everything that lodges in the heart and demands expression. Only when the sentence is understood in this way is its destructiveness and greatness realised. It does not pass over the cultic distinction between clean and unclean but it gives it a new, "eschatological" significance. There are no longer clean and unclean things, there are men clean or unclean "in heart"; and clean is equivalent to good, and unclean to evil.

One might well ask whether this means that a new ethical statute has replaced a cultic one. It is this ostensible replacement which constitutes the real problem of the sentence, for the saying does not simply, as it were, erect a partition between what was formerly prescribed as holy and the moral demand now made, it actually implies that only the morally good is really holy. But how can the two be compared? We recall that Jewish cultic thinking in no sense neglected the demand for morally good behaviour, we think also of the condemnation of all cult on the lips of countless prophets. Jesus, too, used Hosea's word: "I desire steadfast love and not sacrifice." The old opposition, ever so lively, is still there; it is implied in Jesus' word and flames forth with a fury which reduces the cultic commandments to dust and ashes and at the same time lends lustre to the glory of the heart-revealing absoluteness of the moral commandment. And yet there is a difference between the position of the prophets and the position of Jesus. It might be expressed in this way. The prophets say: "don't worry about being clean, be good"; Jesus says: "to be good *is* to be clean." That means that Jesus' saying involves a different

idea of holiness which is found in goodness of heart. Jesus
wants men to be clean and pure, but the qualification is that
no breath of evil should infect the heart.   There is an obvious
allusion to the beatitude: "blessed are the pure in heart." And
just as the beatitude is eschatological so is the sentence before
us.   The breaking in of the time of eschatological fulfilment
means the suspension of all cultic laws of cleanness and purity.
The only valid law is now "be of a pure heart."

One further comment is necessary on this challenge, so simple
and so immense.   Where pronouncements on Jewish cultic
questions have occurred they have up till now been connected
with the sending of the Son of Man; here, however, we have
such a pronouncement but stated as a general rule similar in
form to Rabbinic axioms and reminiscent in its content of
many prophetic and other contemporary sayings.   The
dualism involves no incompatibility, however, any more than
the coming of the Kingdom of God and the presence of the
Son of Man does.   The two stand in the closest possible
relationship to one another: "if it is by the finger of God that I
cast out demons, then the kingdom of God has come upon
you."   A word on the cult can either be expressed as an axiom
if it is the Kingdom of God itself that is being stressed, or it can
be expressed as a revelatory personal word if it is the "person"
of Him who is the Son of Man that is being stressed.   In other
words when the Son of Man wishes to reveal Himself then all
words about cult are brought into relation to Himself, His
work, and His coming and are thereby most gloriously illumined: when it is the still hidden Son of Man who is speaking
then His words are directed towards the coming Kingdom of
God, they are similar in form and content to the utterances of
Jewish Scribes and yet shed through the veil of learning an unmistakably eschatological light. All of which means also of course
that there are connexions between the Kingdom of God which
has come near and the contemporary cult similar to those we
have already found between the Son of Man and the cult; the
Kingdom of God is to be understood as the locus and epitome
of the true cult. We shall have more to say about this later.

The cult problem once again confronts us in the account of
Jesus' last days in Jerusalem.   Here in the very shadow, so
to speak, of the holy Jewish Temple a torrent of questions

concerning priesthood and sacrifice breaks forth and there is no attempt to stop it; indeed one might say that the most significant features of these days as Mark portrays them are the assault on the cult and its overthrow by the Gospel, the death of the Son of Man being as it were the final triumph.

In the story of Jesus' entry into Jerusalem (Mk. XI.1-11) the cult motif seems just present and no more; is it after all any more than an account of the extravagant homage paid by an enthusiastic company of pilgrims and others to an honoured and beloved Rabbi? But even if one were satisfied with such an answer—and the acclamation of the people suggests someone other and greater—there remains a number of incidental questions. What is Jesus' destination? "Jerusalem" (Mk. XI.1) is not enough, it is too vague. For Mark does describe how Jesus was acclaimed and how branches were strewn before Him on the way to the city from the Mount of Olives. He does also expressly state that "the Temple" was the intended destination, and that is also topographically confirmed. The Temple lies in the extreme north of the city, and anyone "going into the Temple" from the north would not touch the city proper, only its outskirts. Jesus makes for the Temple in Jerusalem, then; that is not merely an incidental fact, but reveals a profound and careful design. He enters not only as His people's hidden King spoken of by the prophet Zechariah, but also as the Lord of God's Temple, and Mark seems to want to bring this point into prominence when he alone relates that "he went into the Temple . . . and looked round at everything" (XI.11). This is the Lord coming to inspect and take possession of what belongs to Him. Matthew's version makes it perhaps even clearer that the earliest community put this interpretation on the incident. There, on His entry into the Temple, Jesus drives out the merchants and money-changers from their presumptuous position in the outer court; He consecrates it anew as it were, giving sight to the blind and making the lame walk—the unmistakable sign of the breaking in of the *eschaton*—and He receives for that reason the children's praise "Hosanna to the son of David" (XXI.12-17). As son of David He is the bringer of eschatological fulfilment.

Ask another question and the same conclusion is reached—the question, what did Jesus' entry really mean for the jubilant disciples and pilgrims and what did it mean for the Master they cheered? The outward mode of the entry hardly betrays anything of its deeper significance. There is nothing very remarkable about a person riding into Jerusalem on an ass, it is a familiar detail of city life. Only the spreading of palm branches and the cheering of the crowd would make it in any way unusual. They see in Him the founder of the renewed kingdom of David, and therefore recognise in Him "their king" promised by Zechariah. Since outwardly, however, there is nothing in the incident to suggest this deeper significance the Fourth Gospel can state that the disciples did not understand it (XII.16). What shall we say about the significance of the entry for Jesus Himself? It is surely impossible to think of Him as the object of unsolicited and merely tolerated acts of homage; the accounts of the incident in all four Gospels contradict that. Indeed they represent Him as the author and producer of the whole affair, tracing the acquisition of the animal back to Jesus' miraculous knowledge and strange behaviour. The action and the significance of the action are wholly bound up with one another. There remains only this to say: the demonstration on the entry into Jerusalem is on the one hand even for Jesus, merely the more or less usual homage paid to Him as "the prophet from Nazareth of Galilee" (Mt. XXI.11); it is on the other hand also the fulfilment of the Zechariah prophecy with which the hour of the eschatological fulfilment strikes. There is therefore a dualism involved in the entry as there is in the entrant. As the Hidden One He enters like any other honoured Rabbi; as Son of Man, however, He enters with the secret glory of the King, coming to His people. And here is a new element that exceeds the limits of ancient prophecy: this entry leads to the Temple. The Temple is therefore the place where the secret of the formerly hidden Son of Man is to be unfolded and eschatological fulfilment is to begin. He is therefore the eschatological Lord of this Temple, at once King and High Priest with just such dual honours as Daniel saw in his vision. Under cover of this triumphal entry, therefore, it becomes evident just how closely the presence of the Son of Man and the fact of the Temple are bound up with one another. The next story, as if by way of example, proves these points beyond question.

In the great narrative of the Cleansing of the Temple we see together as in a mirror all the cult questions we have so far discussed, and it is as if there was added light in the reflexion. We must examine them more carefully therefore. All four Gospels report that Jesus drove all the merchants and money-changers out of the sanctuary and thereby made the "den of robbers" into a "house of prayer" again. This fact is in itself remarkable. We see Jesus by word and deed ministering to the needs of men—needs both of body and of soul, we see Him call disciples and fortify them in countless ways for their work; but always in such instances His concern is for men and women and their immediate problems, never for an established holy institution. Similarly where Jesus departs from the prescribed observance of the Sabbath His main concern is not to indicate His approval or disapproval of Sabbath laws, but merely to come to the assistance of man in his distress. In this case, however, it is a question of rescuing a Jewish holy place from misuse and profanation. The remarkable general character of the story is matched by the equally remarkable substance of the incident itself. It is worth trying to imagine the scene. Here we have a court-area of vast extent, so vast that it was one of the marvels of the ancient world. Here we have one man sweeping from it all the hucksters and money-changers, of whom there were enough to fill the place with their noisy business. And there was no resistance and no Temple police on the scene, as when later Peter healed the lame man (Acts IV.4) and the incident completely escaped the notice even of the Roman Guard stationed in the nearby Antonia fort. Nor is the difficulty resolved by reference to the disciples, for we are nowhere told that they assisted Jesus. The writer of the Fourth Gospel thinks of them as amazed spectators (II.17). Jesus accomplishes this thing alone, and by a seemingly irresistible action purges the outer court of the Temple. His power is therefore not human power, rather it is to be explained, as the Fourth Gospel explains it, in a quotation from the Psalms: "zeal for thy house will consume me." His action is therefore, as elsewhere His word is, an action "with power," "with authority" (Mk. 1.22), and therefore an action of God here and now. The non-human element is not to be treated superficially, however; it is the sphere in which the Master, as if self-sufficiently, lives and works and is yet at the same time eclipsed by One Greater: "and he taught," as if this mighty deed He had done could only find its goal and its fulfilment in the mightier Word.

We are still, however, on the story's outer edge. What really was the purpose of Jesus' action? The ground on which the Temple stood was holy, and there were countless provisions for preserving it from even the slightest profanation (cf. Mk. xi.16). Many of them were based on the Torah, the majority stemmed from the exegetical tradition which was entrusted to the priests. Priests, however, had also arranged for the sale of sacrificial animals in the Temple precincts and for the exchange of foreign currency for the old holy temple-money. Annas, the father-in-law of Caiaphas, owned a stall there selling doves, which afforded him a considerable income. But even though abuses of this kind could easily creep in the priestly concession was not affected, and the right established by these arrangements, which did facilitate cultic observance for many pilgrims, was not withdrawn. Besides it was not in the court where pious Jews performed their devotions that this business was allowed but in the so-called Court of the Gentiles, which was separated by a high partition from the holier parts of the Temple. One might almost say that the Court of the Gentiles corresponds to an enclosed church square which one traverses in order to reach the house of God. One should, however, keep in mind that on one side of it, in the direction of the Sanhedrin house, there was to be found the holy foundation stone laid by God, shutting off the underworld and ensuring the permanence of God's house. This was regarded as the centre of the holy land and of the whole world. It is from this place that Jesus clears all din of marketing; He infringes thereby the valid instructions of the Temple authorities and claims in support of His action a holier right than they posses. By what right then does Jesus precipitate the conflict?

We know of purists—particularly it would appear in Galilee —who longed for the day when everything profane should be excluded from the holy precincts of the Temple and the mountain of the Lord. For the most part they were the sworn enemies of the Sadducees, who freely syncretised holy law and human political or mercenary endeavour. The purists could

only find justification for their opposition to this in the contrast
between the holiness of long ago to which the Scriptures
bore witness, and the unholiness of their own day.
Pious *laudatores temporis acti*, they tended to reject the present
in favour of an eagerly anticipated future which would re-
associate the nation's end and fulfilment with its holy beginning.
One might expect to find those elements particularly among
that circle of devout people so impressively described by Luke
in the stories of Simeon and Anna. But the information about
them is scant and vague; and even if it were more precise how
would it help the understanding of our story? Jesus would
then have been the chief agent of a movement of reform aimed
at securing the unconditional holiness of the Temple. And is
it likely that He would have accomplished it in dealing with
an insignificant irregularity in the Court of the Gentiles? Is it
likely that He would have left aside all the more important
questions such as the holiness of the priesthood and the bloody
sacrifice, and have been content with the action alone without
any follow-up? Indeed all this is so improbable that it scarcely
merits more careful refutation. We must rather examine the
text itself.

According to the first three Gospels Jesus appeals to the
prophetic saying:"my house shall be called a house of prayer for
all peoples." The quotation is from Trito-Isaiah in a passage
containing eschatological promises; it speaks not of a definition
of the existing Temple, which would govern the historical life
and attitude of the nation, but of a name which God will one
day give to His chosen house. The existing sacrifices and
prayers, services and blessings of the Temple are perhaps
directed towards that ultimate end indicated by God (more
frequently they diverge from it) but the eschatological reality,
in terms of which this place would become the place for the
worship of God, is not yet there. When God brings the time
of fulfilment for world and people, then His house will be called
"a house of prayer," in the same way as the peacemakers shall
be called "sons of God" (Mt. v.9). The word-for-word
quotation loses nothing of its eschatological meaning on Jesus'
lips; if anything it gains. According to the narrative, therefore,
Jesus bases His action on the idea of the eschatological holiness
of the Temple. He makes preparation for it by removing

everything which militates against that eschatological holiness. But what does it mean to understand the cleansing of the Temple as an act of eschatological preparation?

It is really not the Temple in the strict sense which is "cleansed"; there is no mention of the Temple proper, the various altars and open courts and all the holy equipage. Jesus "cleanses" the outer Court of the Gentiles. That means from a Jewish point of view He purges the outermost approach to the Temple and pays no heed to those places which to the nation and to each individual are of greatest and holiest significance. To be sure the fact that there was a Court of the Gentiles constituted a serious question for the faithful and a devout hope—the question "whât of the night," how long would the "night" of heathendom oppress the people of God (Is. xxi.1), and the hope that one day the nations of the world would come to worship God at Jerusalem. But the hope was still merely a dream, and the question had gone for centuries unanswered. Jesus therefore had done something empty and insignificant, seen from the point of view of the devout Jew. When we view this "cleansing" in the eschatological light shed by Isaiah's prophecy, however, we begin to see it rather differently. What was previously only promise, becomes now a reality drawing near; no, more than that, a reality that has drawn near: from the point of view of the nations of the earth the place for prayer destined by God for them is being made ready. It is no particular bias which makes Mark the only one of the Evangelists to quote the Isaiah text in full; even if Matthew and Luke omit the words "for all peoples," to anyone who knew the text, and particularly in view of the surroundings, the meaning could hardly be in doubt. In the cleansing of the Temple we are concerned only indirectly with a Jewish Temple problem and much more directly with the problem of the "Gentiles."

The problem occurs also in Jesus' preaching ministry and is never clearly resolved. Alongside the instruction to the disciples, "go nowhere among the Gentiles," there is the promise that "many will come from east and west and sit at table with Abraham, Isaac, and Jacob in the kingdom of heaven" (Mt. x.5, viii.1). Alongside journeys and ministry in Galilee there are journeys and ministry in heathen territory, and there is

D

the revelation on a "heathen" hill, the Mount of Trans-
figuration, besides the other revelation on a hill called
Calvary, the hill of His death. Above all the word connected
with the cup at the Last Supper is relevant for it speaks of a
covenant "for the many," or to be more precise and again
in words reminiscent of Isaiah, of "blood, shed for many"
(cf. Is. LIII.12), i.e. for the nations of the earth. This word and
the action in the Temple both yield the same lesson: the problem of the nation is an eschatological problem and belongs
in all its parts to the greater event which brings fulfilment for
the nation and the nations. This event equally is coming and
has come, the signs of it are everywhere apparent in the work
and preaching of Jesus. Likewise eschatological salvation is
coming to the nations, and yet the Master's life's work is confined
and directed to His own nation. In this larger context Jesus'
action appears as one of exemplary clarity; it takes place in
the sanctuary of the Jewish people and takes place therein for
the benefit of the Gentiles. For that reason it can ignore what
the Jews would consider the essential constituents of the House
of God, the daily sacrifice and the unceasing priestly service.
Sacrifice and priesthood were truly God's gifts to the people,
but they were intended only for the period of its earthly
pilgrimage; at the end and in the fulfilment both will cease
and the whole people will be a "kingdom of priests." In
history the people is separated from the peoples by sacrifice
and priesthood, at the end both shall be united by prayer and
thanksgiving and God's house will be called a house of prayer
for all peoples. Consider too that here in the Temple of
Jerusalem is the sacred centre of all peoples and of the whole
world. When one interprets the narrative in this way as
portraying an eschatological sign of the presence of the last
times, then it takes place in the same context as the acts of
healing or of the calling of the disciples to be eschatological
judges. Now is the time of eschatological preparedness. That
explains why the conflict with the ecclesiastical laws and
usages of the Temple authorities is completely disregarded.
This is infinitely more important. Jesus by His action has
removed the hindrance to the fulfilment of the reality of the
Temple as a house of prayer for all peoples.
  We cannot then avoid the question by what authority Jesus

acted as He did, and it is easily answered. As His acts of healing
were done in virtue of His authority as Son of Man, at once
hiding and revealing in human work the signs of God's eschatological work of fulfilling, so also this cleansing of the Temple
court is done in virtue of the power and authority of the
eschatological Son of Man and is a sign of the "kingdom of
heaven at hand." It is also claimed that it belongs to the Son
of Man to consecrate these places anew. In other words the
Son of Man is not only the Lord who rescues men in their
times of misfortune and need, He also frees men from sin and
uncleanness; and therefore He is Lord of the Temple and
fulfiller of its purpose or, as the Gospel of Mark has it, and it
is the first name given to Him there, He is the "Holy One of
God," with power over whatever in the world is holy.

We can be even more precise concerning this general
eschatological interpretation. Jesus' action impugns Jewish
priestly and national institutions—"you have made it a den of
robbers." We cannot really determine to whom the words
are addressed; it is sufficient that Jesus hurls them at men
listening to Him. There is also no indication given why the
trade in sacrificial animals and currency is so reprehensible,
who has profaned the Temple court or exactly how. There is
simply the unmistakable fact that in Jesus' action the old
prophetic word is fulfilled and the Master has therefore the
right and the power to restore the thing profaned by men to
its original, God-given, eschatological purpose. All this is
justified, however, only if it belongs of right to Jesus as the Son
of Man to set Himself against the current practice of the cult,
without any consideration of questions of guilt or guilty, and
to give effect to the real idea of the eschatological cult, the idea
of the Temple as a "house of prayer for all peoples." Because
He is the Son of Man and has such authority He can attack
what is permitted and call it robber-like, and describe as "a
den of robbers" that which despite all obscuring still retains
for Jewish faith the light of the holiness of God. And yet to
a great degree in every revealing act there is hiddenness, in
every attack there is still preserved the concern of the Son of
Man for His people; He remains the Hidden One in that He
consecrates "only" the place where the Gentiles should worship
God, He remains also the loving Lord in that He turns His

attention to the wandering and ensnared of heathendom and
leaves God's holy place untouched for the Jewish people. In
a sense, however, the silence is as eloquent an arraignment as
the word about the "den of robbers." The Jewish people had
excluded from the worship of God those whom it was the very
purpose of the eschatological sending of the Son of Man "to
call"—we may now so put it. That is their sin, that is their
robbery from the nations, that they have appropriated what
God promised them, the house where they could pray to
God, the house which is for one people and for all peoples,
always, however, God's House. The task of Jesus as Son of
Man is to work for the House of God: that means "yes" to the
cult where it is in agreement with the will of God, "no" to the
cult where it is not in agreement with His will. The Son of
Man's task is fulfilled as eschatological reality where He lives
and holds bridal celebration with His own, the wanderers and
the sinners.

One may now perhaps realise more fully the profundity of
the reasoning behind the placing of this eschatological act in the
Fourth Gospel among its opening narratives, whereas the
other three have placed it at the beginning of their accounts of
the last days in Jerusalem. It is equivalent to the cry: "the
kingdom of heaven is at hand." But indeed both in the Fourth
Gospel and in the Synoptics the position of the story is governed
by theology rather than by history, the theology of the particular Evangelist. It should not therefore be a surprise to
learn that no trace of this event is found in extra-biblical
history covering the period of Jesus' last days. In itself, seen
through the eyes of the authorities, it is merely an oversight on
the part of the police, an incident of no great significance
compared with the more dangerous character of the whole
movement and its leader. For the early community of
believers, on the other hand, criteria of history meant nothing.
They saw only the secret greatness of the incident, what is
proclaimed and what it also made real. The problem of the
cult that Jesus has grasped and solved continues therefore to
dominate the following chapter.

In the chapters of Mark that follow the account of the
incident we have been examining, there begins that great
controversy in which one opponent after another leaves the

arena vanquished; and the arena is the newly sanctified Court of the Gentiles with the gilded spires of the Temple proper glinting through its enclosing columns. In this great court He encounters first the "chief priests and the Scribes and the elders." Their question is: "by what authority are you doing these things?" The little word "these" in Mark and Matthew can refer only to the recent cleansing of the Temple, and the reference is very significant. The question presumes the presence here of the same authority as that by which Jesus on other occasions taught and acted, and as the acts of healing and the words of proclamation both revealed and hid the eschatological messenger of God, so also this act stands, so to speak, in the same twilight of an eschatological dawn. Even if the question is the early Church's question and merely put by them on the lips of Jesus' opponents, nevertheless the question reveals the keenness of their understanding which could carry them away beyond all external questions and consequences of this conflict to the revelatory authority of their Lord. Also Jesus' counter-question about the baptism of John gains in perspicacity and colour, for this baptism is not merely the historical starting-point, nor yet merely the eschatological basis for Jesus' ministry of healing and proclamation; baptism and Temple-cleansing have a much closer connexion. If we consider the baptism of John as the beginning of an eschatological alternative to Jewish sacrifice, then Jesus' action in cleansing the Temple is taking the step which John did not take. John presented an alternative but he left the original standing; Jesus changes the original and sanctifies it in accordance with its original destiny and its original prophetic reference to the time of fulfilment, which the Jewish priesthood had failed to appreciate and had indeed completely distorted. The whole scene is outwardly an argument in the Rabbinic manner, only it is not rabbis who argue in well-matched rivalry. What is really happening, historically speaking, is that the highest authorities of the Jewish people are calling to account Him who has so arbitrarily interfered with their rights. When, however, the Gospels tell that Jesus repulsed His adversaries and triumphed over them it is because in the writers' view He was the true Lord and keeper of the Temple while the chief priests and their followers were corrupt and

outrageous usurpers. Confirmation of all this, proof that we
are not guilty of reading into the story what is not there, comes
in the parable of the Wicked Husbandmen which follows
immediately the passage we have been examining.

It is customary to interpret the parable along the lines of
Isaiah v, whence the first few clauses are undoubtedly bor-
rowed, and to explain the vineyard as the Jewish people, whom
God has "planted" as His own people. The parable thereafter
loses its inner coherence altogether in the strait-jacket of the
traditional interpretation. Is there any parallel between ruler
and people and tenant and vineyard? How could a husband-
man really suppose he could appropriate the property he
managed by maltreating his master's messengers and killing
his only son? All these inner improbabilities point to another
interpretation, consciously diverging from Isaiah v and not
difficult to find amongst the material to hand. The vineyard
is not God's people but His House (with all it implies), the holy
Temple. The profound, fiercely polemical meaning of the
parable is that the priests are the tenants of God's sanctuary,
and it is then strikingly true that the servants of God and of
His sanctuary are the designing usurpers who drive off the
messengers of the true Lord and kill His son and heir. Therefore
the lord of the vineyard "will . . . give the vineyard to others"
(Mk. xii.9). We scarcely require to point out how closely this
element of the parable connects with Jesus' action in the
Temple. In such an interpretation also it is clearly relevant
that a golden vine adorned the Temple as a sign and symbol
of its belonging to God; one might almost think the parable
was a new creation using the motifs of this emblem and the
Isaianic metaphor. Admittedly this conception implies that
the Temple at Jerusalem was more than the headquarters of
the Jewish cult, but the truth of this very implication is well
warranted in Holy Scripture for every pious Jew, and Jesus
Himself by His act of cleansing had borne new witness to it.
The Temple is the one place for the true worship of God and
the abiding security for the coming eschatological fulfilment.
In the light of this parable, and also of Jesus' action in the
Temple, this means that at and in the sanctuary of God there
is revealed the Kingdom of God. Since this Temple is God's
gift and His foundation it is also the operative form of the

Kingdom of God in history, the form which will be fulfilled in the time of the end. Again, however, since it is in history and has been misused by men it is the exact opposite of the Kingdom of God and as such must be destroyed. Some kind of compromise between these two apparently irreconcilable patterns is perhaps offered in the parable before us, for it views even the existing "vineyard" as epitome and essence of the Kingdom of God of the end-time. The gap is bridged by the idea that this Kingdom of God is itself a holy temple, *the* House of God.

This parable alone of all the others speaks of the "son and heir," and that is not accidental. It is not only the objective Kingdom of God which is to be revealed at the sanctuary of God but also the person of the Son of Man, He who is the Holy One of God, the Lord and Keeper of the eschatological temple. There is profound significance in the quotation from Isaiah, added as if in corroboration, concerning the stone which the builders rejected. It reveals in obviously cultic images what was being said previously in the parable under cover of the vineyard. But it portrays also with more clearly interpretative strokes the fate of Him who is destined to crown the true and holy Temple of God. If the relationship of the vineyard to the "son," of the inheritance to the "heir," was implicit but still indefinite in the parable, now still figuratively but unmistakably we are told of rejection and coronation, and for the Temple's sake. In other words the Temple binds the objective Kingdom of God and the person of the Son of Man together in an indissoluble unity. For the Temple's sake the stone— and to be Son of Man means undoubtedly to be God's cornerstone in His Temple—is rejected and exalted. Now it becomes clearer why no reference is ever made to the priesthood or lordship of Jesus in the Temple. Both do belong to one another, but in such a way that so long as the Son of Man preserves His secret He belongs to the Temple and only when He has disclosed the secret does the Temple belong to Him. From a new and unexpected direction it becomes clear, therefore, that the purpose and glory of the mission of the Son of Man will be revealed, in life as in death, at the Temple.

The Lucan version of the saying (xx.17-18) makes this last point perhaps even clearer. Luke adds to his quotation from

Ps. cxviii.23 a further reference which borrows from Dan. ii.34 and ii.44:

Every one who falls on that stone will be broken to pieces; but when it falls on any one it will crush him.

These lines present a slightly different picture from that in the quotation from the psalm. Even in the Old Testament, however, foundation-stone and corner-stone are often confused; the former means the holy rock on which the building stands, the latter means the crowning stone above the portal. What Daniel says of the rock is here in Luke ascribed also to the corner-stone: it is cut out from its place and breaks in pieces all upon whom it falls. And again this corner-stone is as immovably set in position as the rock that holds up the Temple; none of its assailants—which may even include "the gates of Hades" (Mt. xvi.18)—will prevail against it: they will be dashed in pieces. Who this corner-stone is cannot be in dispute, nor is the change really so extraordinary whereby the One who elsewhere is called the builder of the Temple becomes a "stone." In the Old Testament God is likewise both the builder of the sanctuary and the rock on which it is built. This kind of thing is quite common. Jesus consecrates the Temple at Jerusalem as the eschatological place of prayer and also threatens that He will destroy it. Jesus knows He is sent "unto the lost sheep of the house of Israel;" He also proclaims that "the sons of the Kingdom shall be cast forth into the outer darkness." The Kingdom of God, according to the parable of the Vinedresser, has already come in former times and therefore really exists: it will also come as something entirely new and different. In all these examples past divine acts of an historical nature are ranged over against the events of the eschatological fulfilment in apparent conflict, but it is merely the same conflict that is present in the person of the Master. He is God's messenger at the end of His people's history like other divine messengers before Him, and He is at the same time the "Son," the heir of the vineyard; He is both stone and builder.

In the subsequent controversies the argument does not directly refer to cultic questions; but not infrequently the Temple atmosphere affects the trend of the argument, and of

course the broad forecourt of the Temple remains the eschatologically prepared place where the last agents of error and
confusion still operate. The question of tribute provides a
good example. It is a burning problem for the Jewish people,
not really because as a freedom-loving people they resent
paying tax to a foreign and heathen conqueror, but rather
because it is their privilege to pay taxes only to the Temple and
therefore to God. Jesus' great answer ignores the priestly
prerogative altogether, as if it did not exist, and requires only
that what is God's should be given to God.

In the discussion on the resurrection of the dead we may
confine ourselves to noting the bluntness of the rebuff and the
vehemence of the retort: "you know neither the scriptures nor
the power of God" (Mk. XII.24). Between the priestly Sadducee
party who are here the questioners and Jesus there is no connecting link, only inexorable opposition. The significance of the
cultic element in the question concerning the greatest commandment is therefore considerably greater in this kind of
context. It is one of the most superb and profound pictures in
the whole Marcan gallery. Within the holy Temple area, even
within sight of the reeking altars themselves, the complete
overthrow of sacrifice and Temple is proclaimed—"to love
God . . . and . . . his neighbour as oneself is much more than
all whole burnt offerings and sacrifices." Man does not
require any particular holy sacrifice or mediation of priests, or
Jewish nationality; his relationship to God is determined not
by what he gives to God at a holy place but by whether or not
he loves God in his neighbour. The point is doubly made and
most concretely here in Mark. One will find in the Old Testament expressions of this idea of love over against sacrifice
and the old prophetic attack: "I desire steadfast love
and not sacrifice." By comparison, however, this matter
of loving God and one's neighbour as oneself covers a
vastly greater area, an area which rabbinic exegesis did
indeed sometimes explore but which had certainly never
before been so straightforwardly and daringly made the sole
basis of the relationship between God and man. And there is
more; the phrase "more than all whole burnt offerings and
sacrifices" brings to mind so many analogous sayings: "more
than the sanctuary, more than a prophet, than Jonah, than

Solomon." The eschatological perfection of Him who can make such statements is unmistakable. One will understand this "more" therefore in the sense suggested and indeed confirmed by Jesus' words of commendation, "You are not far from the Kingdom of God." "Burnt offerings and sacrifices" are still offered, but something higher by far has appeared in time which is indeed merely the ancient holy legacy handed down. In the consummated Kingdom of God only these two things matter and the two things are really one thing: loving God with one's whole heart and one's neighbour as oneself. Thus a relative, i.e. a historical, validity is still conceded to the cult and in the same breath it is absolutely, i.e. eschatologically superseded. It would be easy to go on hearing cultic echoes of greater or lesser clarity in the subsequent snatches of narrative. In the question about the son of David we remember the word: "Thou art a priest for ever"; in the story of the poor widow casting her alms into the treasury we recall that it was placed in the forecourt of the Temple. But such echoes are lost in the fury of sound with which the Apocalyptic Discourse lashes forth against the Temple. Here we no longer encounter historical tensions and contemporary human opponents; here we are dealing with the decisive eschatological battles of the near future, and the target is the Temple. The sanctuary which formerly was the one true abode of God and of His worship becomes now the accursed stronghold of Antichrist. It becomes the place of the Devil's triumph but also of final destruction:

There will not be left here one stone upon another, that will not be thrown down.

One gathers from such apocalyptic images that for Jesus, or else for the early community, the Temple and all its works represented the last enemy of God and of Him whom He sent. And the grounds for this antagonism are purely eschatological. On account of the urgency of the eschatological event the antagonism also directly determines Jesus' whole attitude to His life and His death.

Coming after such a climax the Passion narrative seems to have only its own unfathomable profundity and to have no connexions with cult questions. And yet the motifs we have discovered in other parts of Mark are recognisable here too.

They are even, as it were, clarified and more exactly defined
by reason of the very magnitude of the events. The story
of the Passion is also after all the story of a Passover which
Jesus celebrated in solemnity and suffering, in agony and death;
by the festive hours of the Passover the cruel hours of this
Passion are numbered. Those who prepare this (Jesus')
Passover are priests; they contrive His death, they hire the
traitor, they dispatch the arresting party composed of their
own servants, they examine Him and abuse Him, they incite
the people to demand His crucifixion, and they mock Him on
the cross. All this is the priests' doing, and illustrates with
what implacable hatred the chief priests pursued Jesus, with
what abhorrence also the narrators, the early community,
regarded their Master's arch-enemies and murderers. This
deadly enmity was no doubt occasioned by the historical
situation which made the chief priests the judges and disposers
of Jesus' fate, but its intensity also surely points to the true,
deeper reasons for it in terms of which the priests become the
incarnation of devilish powers fighting against God's one true
envoy.

Apart altogether from these outward circumstances, however,
cultic ideas do three times affect the inner significance of
events, at the beginning, in the middle, and at the end of the
Passion. At the beginning we have the story of the preparation
of the Passover meal. We shall leave aside the question
whether Jesus' last evening with His disciples really was a
Passover evening; if the dating in the Synoptic tradition is in
fact a day out—as I think probable—then the Passover-
colouring of the events in the minds of the community is all
the more striking. Jesus Himself has the evening celebration
prepared by two of His disciples, and one gains some idea of
the importance of this preparation to the community in their
recollection from the fact that the story goes to the trouble of
including the miracle that was employed to find and get ready
the place for the feast. Nor is it an insignificant miracle such
as a favoured prophet or teacher might have performed, it is
a miracle of the same order as that which preceded Jesus'
entry into Jerusalem, a miracle which revealed not only His
wonderful foreknowledge but also and with incontrovertible
accuracy the secret of His kingly stature. It was so important

to the Master to celebrate the Passover with His disciples that
He took up the preparation of it into the miracle side of His
person. Nevertheless of all the various preparations which the
pious use and wont of the times demanded, only one is mentioned and it constitutes the entire content of the story:
"where is my guest room, where I am to eat the Passover with
my disciples?" (XIV.14). Only the place for a celebration is
determined and prepared; all the other things which are
almost more important for the celebration of a Passover—the
procuring and slaughtering of the lamb, the preparation of the
vegetables, the bread, the wine, and whatever else pertains to
festivity—all of this is passed over in silence or concealed in the
general and, as we shall see, ambiguous phrase, "and they
prepared the passover." But what significance is there in
Jesus' fulfilling here an ancient cultic injunction according to
the strictest requirements of pious usage if on other occasions
He neglected them or consciously transgressed them?

The next two narratives, especially that of the Last Supper,
explain the matter adequately; certain difficult questions of
literary arrangement enter here, but we can leave them unanswered since we are concerned only to grasp the essential
content of the tradition which the Evangelist had before him.
At the point in the story where according to Jewish custom the
Passover feast would come, there appears instead the announce-
ment of the betrayal and Jesus' last meal with His disciples.
In other words the Jewish festival is consciously, or unconsciously, "christianised." It is emptied of its traditional
content and given a new one that depends entirely on the
Master's word and work. The new thing which here takes
place becomes the basis and essence of an early Christian
Passover celebration—hence the miraculous and mysterious
preparation. But what a contrast and how completely new
the atonement it contains! The early Christian community's
antipathy to the Jewish cult is so vehement and irreconcilable
that it dissociates itself from the greatest and holiest of
Jewish festivals, the festival celebrating the mighty act of God
in founding His people, and His promise to bring for them in
the future, near or distant, a time of fulfilment. And yet this
abandonment is not complete, for if the new content given by
the Master involves preparation as for a Jewish Passover

celebration—the ambiguity of the phrase "and they prepared the passover" is now resolved—it means that those who humbly followed the example of their Master and Lord did observe a new kind of loyalty to this old and sacred tradition. Just as He denied the validity of the traditional cult and immediately proceeded to recognise it again as the prophetic pointer to the eschatological cult, so here the traditional holy custom of preparation is retained and fulfilled in the Master's miracle. He Himself makes the transition to that which lay dormant and prophetic at the root of the old Passover festival and now in the Lord's Supper becomes living eschatological reality. There is only a slight difference between Jesus' attitude and that of the tradition behind this Gospel; the latter already sees, hardened into new cultic usages, what for Jesus was the visible sign in word and action, a sign that could and must be fulfilled, but the visible sign of an eschatological reality, an eschatological present. That perhaps helps to explain why it was so important for the Synoptic tradition that this first and oldest celebration of the Supper should be seen to be rooted in the preparation customs of the Passover.

We shall consider later the cultic content of the Lord's Supper and likewise the cultic associations which after this great beginning continue in the middle of the Passion narrative. The proceedings before the Sanhedrin revolve around the great cultic "witness":

I will destroy this temple that is made with hands, and in three days I will build another.

They reach their climax in the starkest of all oppositions, that of the High Priest Caiaphas talking of blasphemy and the captive Jesus confessing Himself the Son of Man, and it ends significantly with the gross ill-usage which He suffers silently at the hands of the members of the Sanhedrin and their servants.

One last astonishing piece of narrative at the end of the Gospel belongs to the same context, the narrative describing the many signs which accompanied Jesus' death. And even if several of them are also found in ancient religion at the departing of a divine favourite, and others are foreshadowed in Old Testament prophecy, such conjectures as to their origin do not relieve us of the task of asking what these elements in

the story of Jesus' death mean. Matthew relates that "many
bodies of the saints who had fallen asleep were raised, and
coming out of the tombs after His resurrection they went into
the holy city and appeared to many" (xxvii.52f.). The hour
of Jesus' death therefore marks the beginning of resurrection
and of eschatological fulfilment. The darkness over the whole
earth in Mark's account is equally significant, corresponding
as it does to that apocalyptic eclipse of sun and moon in Mk.
xiii.24f. Among all these signs of the end of the world one
predominates: "And the curtain of the Temple was torn in
two, from top to bottom," or as the Gospel of the Hebrews has
it, "the lintel carrying the corner-stone of the Temple broke."
These two things undoubtedly have the same meaning—Jesus'
end is also the end of the Temple. God has destroyed that
which seemed built to last for ever, and laid bare that which
by its holy destiny was to remain always in unapproachable
darkness. Thus in the Master's death there was a consummation of His life work—the Jewish cult was nullified. We
may also presume to know the reason for the annullment. The
Master's death was the last and greatest work towards which
His mission was directed. It became the work and the hour of
eschatological fulfilment.

We have reached the end of Mark's Gospel and it has
afforded abundant material for our problem. It would no
doubt be possible to collect further evidence from the rest of
the Gospel tradition, especially from the Fourth Gospel which
in its whole presentation is very much influenced by cultic
considerations, as the position of the Cleansing of the Temple
at the beginning of the Gospel itself shows. But we must leave
this material aside; the necessary task of distinguishing between
tradition and production in the Fourth Gospel would involve
us in matters far beyond the scope of the present study. The
first and third Gospels also contain a considerable amount of
cultic matter which we shall now briefly examine because it
can help to throw into bolder relief the exceptional quality of
Mark's tradition.

In Matthew's Gospel we note first of all the angel's word to
Joseph, announcing the child's name (1.21):

You shall call His name Jesus, for He will save His people from their sins.

The sentence is all the more instructive in that in the promised birth there is fulfilled both an Old Testament prophecy and an Old Testament name from which shines forth all the glory of the time of eschatological fulfilment: "Emmanuel" (which means God, with us)." Through the Child and His subsequent work is realised the great hope that at the end of days God would dwell constantly with His people. Such a sentence, however, raises the problem of the cult; for where is the dwelling of God at the moment if not in the Temple, and how is the work of saving from sin effected if not through the priestly sin-offering? It is characteristic of this promise that it observes a complete silence about these God-given places and media of salvation, and concentrates on the final complete salvation and the Saviour of the end-time who is to be born in this child Jesus. The other thing is that the child's work is going to be saving His people from their sins. The sending of the Son of Man is thus described in almost the same words as Jesus uses in His exchange with the Scribes (Mk. II.10): "But that you may know that the Son of Man has authority on earth to forgive sins." And eschatological fulfilment here is so closely bound up with saving from sin that all other hopes contained in the Jewish faith—hopes for peace and dominion, for the unity and indestructibility of the Jewish people, and all other expressions of religio-nationalistic expectation—vanish like a puff of earthly smoke before the heavenly light of forgiveness of sin. Significantly also the sentence reads "His people," not "the people." In other words His work is not directed towards a historically given community but towards a community arising eschatologically, which He founds and makes "His people." This is a basic element of the story, an element we have encountered here and there already. It is no longer cult but Old Testament prophecy interpreted eschatologically which governs the life and work of Jesus in which the time of eschatological fulfilment dawns.

We must allude only in passing to the story of Jesus' temptation. It relates without the slightest sign of surprise what for Jewish eyes and ears is simply blasphemous—that the Devil set foot on the pinnacle of the Temple as though God's house was at his disposal. No respect is given to the special sanctity of the place, the pinnacle of the Temple is no more than a lofty,

somewhat dangerous, vantage-point commanding an extensive
view in Jewry's midst—no reverence here for the traditional
and jealously guarded holiness of the Temple! Perhaps the
basis of this disrespect and complete disregard may be detected
in the introduction to Jesus' ministry peculiar to Matthew's
Gospel (IV.15-16 after Is. IX.1-2): Capernaum and Galilee of
the Gentiles have become through the Master God's eschatological holy places and the Temple at Jerusalem the seat of the
Devil.

Certain elements which characterise the whole Gospel are
still more important; a few examples may suffice. Mark, it
will be remembered, began his account of Jesus' work of
healing with the story of a casting out of a demon; Matthew
begins with the healing of a leper, then of a Gentile, and next
of a woman. They are persons who were either excluded from
the Jewish cult or assigned a subordinate place within it.
Time and again Matthew emphasises that the eschatological
community of the called is the community of the sick and the
suffering, the halt and the lame; the "healthy" belong to the
people of Israel. The difference between the two is expressed
in the quotation from Hosea: "I desire mercy and not sacrifice"
(IX.13). In the story of the disciples plucking the ears of grain,
the first Evangelist really collates three *logia* which are directed
against Temple and priests and which in Matthew's own words
amount to, "something greater than the temple is here."
Emphasis on this "something greater," this eschatological
superiority of Gospel over cult, is a feature of Matthew's
record. It is very marked in the account of Jesus' entry into
Jerusalem. A brilliant eschatological mantle incorporating
old and new threads is cast around the Master on His modest
progress. The jubilant prophecy of Zechariah stands out
boldly, the city is stirred by the whole incomprehensible affair,
and then the entry is crowned by a dramatic Temple trilogy:
the forecourt is cleansed of the tables of the hucksters and
money-changers, there gather around the Master as His
chosen people those who previously had been excluded from
the sacred precincts ("the blind see and the lame walk") and
children's voices break out in a revelry of Hosannas. In all
this Jesus remains the central character, He is the lord and
keeper of the Temple entering it in solemn ceremony, and in

the precincts of the old, newly cleansed sanctuary the new community of the eschatological period is constituted.

In reporting the last days in Jerusalem Matthew has again undoubtedly sharpened the issues. In the Judas narratives the chief priests are no longer merely mortal enemies but also hypocrites, who will not defile themselves with the money which they themselves have set apart for the traitor who is to secure Jesus' death. At the end they become the inventors of the treacherous lie which would make God's eschatological act of fulfilment in Jesus' resurrection a fraud contrived by the disciples. This is further evidence of the bitter battles waged by priests and Temple representatives against the life and the death of the Master.

The underlying attitude of Matthew's Gospel to the problem of Temple and cult is perhaps most clearly revealed in the story of the Temple tax, which is found only in this Gospel. The superficial point of the story is to present Jesus as winner by His clever handling of the question of the paying of tax. Nevertheless this is not the real marvel, not even according to the record: the real marvel is the teaching for audience and reader contained in Jesus' answer. If one pays tax one is subject to the body levying the tax; was the Master then also subject to the Temple? The story provides a double answer. The comparison with the practice of earthly rulers transfers the problem to the context of "weltlichen Ordnung" (worldly order) to use a Lutheran expression; the Temple tax is not the wages of heaven but an earthly due. But then there is a second answer in the significant contrast drawn between sons and others (XVII.25), which when applied to the question of Temple tax would mean: if a man pays tax he is a stranger to the Lord of the Temple. The tax, which according to the Old Testament guarantees for the faithful Jew his membership of the nation and his right of access to the Temple, is therefore no longer a sign of his being a son of God, it is rather a sign of a servitude to others; and consequently the "sons" are released from all Temple requirements, of which the Temple tax is one. One scarcely requires to emphasise that the struggle for or against the Temple is clearly over if it has become the institution of "others," and if we are not now reckoning with the original difference between heathen and Jews but only with that

E

between sons and "others," i.e. Christians and non-Christians. But the Temple still stands, the tax is still levied and paid, and the tax-collectors still do not distinguish between sons and others. So long as this distinction remains implicit the Temple retains a certain significance. It is not a judicial or religious significance, it is merely a sign of that imperfection which, partaking of this "still," inevitably is at variance with the forward-looking tendencies of the sons and is not conscious of its true nature. As far as the "sons" are concerned, however, the payment of the tax is like a charitable giving of alms, to avoid trouble, so long as the ultimate distinction between sons and others is not yet observed. It will be readily understood that this compromise between eschatological demands and historical situations, between the Lord of the End and the Lord of Time became later extraordinarily helpful in establishing the relationship between religious and historical, or spiritual and worldly order. But it is also clear that the background to our problem here is other than it was in Mark; the period of conflict with Jewish cult is over, and the community has defined its own sphere of action in which its members live unmolested despite their surroundings. A peaceable compromise arrangement exists, its principles dictated for the " sons" by the will of the Master who Himself once voluntarily made His miraculous power serve the ends of just such a compromise.

On the whole the Gospel according to St Matthew is very similar to Mark's Gospel so far as our problem is concerned. Some lines are more firmly drawn, others are blurred or faint, but the basic design remains the same. We breathe a different atmosphere, however, when we enter the Gospel according to St Luke. Many of Jesus' words and actions with cultic relevance in Mark are reproduced—this is the mark of the dutiful chronicler's fidelity, he is bound to what was "delivered to us by those who . . . were eye-witnesses and ministers of the word" (1.2). Wherever this tradition shows a variation of approach, however, Luke's Gospel takes the opportunity to soft-pedal the original opposition to Temple and cult. We need only take note of a few examples. Luke speaks frequently of the reproach for breaking the Sabbath, but nowhere does he report such a radical answer as that given by Matthew ("something greater than the Temple is here"). In Luke's

Gospel Jesus brushes aside the reproach with a quotation of which even rabbis could approve, to the effect that it is more important to help a person in need than to keep the Sabbath holy. The word about clean and unclean, which smashes so violently through all cultic barriers, is suppressed. The cleansing of the Temple is reported, but the account is very brief and concentrates on the main issue—preparation for Jesus' daily teaching of the people in the Temple. In the Apocalyptic Discourse the prophecy about the downfall of the Temple is preserved, but the Temple no longer becomes the stronghold of Antichrist. On the contrary the holy city bears patiently the siege which the nations impose so that even in the last extremity the ancient holiness is preserved. Jesus' great utterance in which He declares that the destruction of the Temple is the object of the Lord's work is omitted, and the rending of the veil of the Temple at the time of Jesus' death is represented as merely one of several frightening omens preceding the event and is therefore robbed of its own particular significance.

Though all the above-mentioned points are negative, the positive approach to the matter which has given rise to them is easily discernible. For Luke's Gospel the Temple remains the place of sacred service and prayer; that can be seen from those narratives that are peculiar to it. Probably one should not make too much of the Temple and priestly atmosphere of the stories of John the Baptist's infancy, as John's parents were of priestly stock; and as if in conscious contrast the narrative of Jesus' nativity is free of all cultic connexions and knows only the marvel of Bethlehem and Nazareth, ordinary saintly folk and shepherds. The situation alters, however, in the subsequent stories in which the Temple is the centre of interest. Mary fulfils the cultic duties required of every Jewish mother, she offers a sacrifice. Nowhere else in all the Gospels do we ever read of such a thing being done. Even more important is the moving picture of the two aged persons waiting for years in the Temple for the consolation of Israel and recognising with gratitude and with grim presentiment the One who would bring salvation and redemption for the people in the child Jesus. The cult is here clearly the providential ground on which grows as its fairest flower Israel's redemption. Its significance and destiny are not in itself but in something coming, to which it points as if with the finger of God, as indeed the whole history of the people from its earliest beginnings has pointed—a fulfilment proffered by God. The Temple is the holy, inherited, divine guarantee of the certainty of the coming salvation. Cult and priesthood are then included within the whole great inheritance which God gradually and invisibly brings to fulfilment, an inheritance in which, alongside the Temple, nation, land, city, Law, and promise all have their place. The only difference between this and the Jewish point of view is that it is not holy priests but faithful people who have experience of the salvation that is at hand. They are the bearers of the prophetic word and of the Holy Ghost; for them the Temple is little more than the place where they pray, the promised place where they will see the Saviour.

The same attitude underlies the well-known story of Jesus at the age of twelve. Again the occasion is a pious observance— a pilgrimage to Jerusalem for the Passover; again, however, we hear little or nothing about the sacred festival itself. The Temple is not the holy place of sacrifice and cult but the house in which God dwells and declares His will, a house of prayer and doctrine for all the devout like any synagogue, even if they do not share the same sanctity. In this story also, therefore, it is not priests who figure but "the teachers." They are the true theologians, familiar with God's Law through long ex- perience of it. And Jesus is a scholar in the school of divine wisdom and therefore "must be in His father's house." The Temple, in which He listens to His people's teachers, is the holy house of God even for Him who in a quite special sense is the Son of God. This is not the picture of the bringer of eschatological fulfilment that we found in Matthew and Mark: as Son of Man and Son of God He is not the destroyer of the old Temple and builder of a new but the duteous son of His people who for all the individuality of His eschatological mission knows He is bound to God's holy dwelling-place. There is no mention here of opposition to the Temple and its priestly service. There is equally, however, no mention of that in virtue of which the sanctuary is most sacred—the daily sacrifice.

One can see this attitude implicit in other narratives even

where there is discernible a certain opposition to the priesthood. The parable of the Good Samaritan, for example, does not castigate priests and Levites as such; it criticises them for failing to include a helpful love of one's neighbour in what they claim is the pattern of the good life, the life that is well pleasing to God. In Matthew the demand was: "I desire mercy and not sacrifice": here it is: "I desire mercy whatever one does about sacrifice." Similarly in the parable of the Pharisee and the publican the Temple is again "merely" the place where each of them enters the presence of God in prayer. There is no suggestion of any offering that would blot out their sin. Indeed on the contrary it says explicitly: "this man went down to his house justified"—and he had only prayed! Sincere prayer has quietly and as of right taken the place of sacrifice. However profound are the real reasons for such a change, there is no supplanting of the Temple as in Matthew and Mark but merely an alteration in its significance—witness the last words of the Gospel: "And they returned to Jerusalem with great joy, and were continually in the Temple blessing God" (xxiv.52-3). The Temple, the ancient sanctuary of the Jewish people, is also for the Christian community the centre of its worship of God and the Lord Jesus Christ.

The nature of our problem in the Synoptics is strange. Matthew and Mark—the former sometimes independently of the latter—represent Jesus as fiercely opposed to Temple and cult and doing battle with them; Luke represents Him as both lord and son of the hereditary sanctuary, acknowledging it both in word and action. It would be intriguing to examine the reasons for these differences in approach to one of the most important questions in Jewish and early Christian religion. The fact itself is, however, for us more important. Indeed we must ask about the fact whether it is so certain, whether there is not an occasional discord in the two different choruses however rich and abundant the voices. We often hear in our day: "the whole Synoptic perspective reckons with both things, with Jesus' acceptance of the Temple worship as the divinely decreed method of honouring God and with His superseding of the Temple."[1] We offer no opinion on whether there is a

---

[1] Schrenk in *Theologisches Wörterbuch zum Neuen Testament*, ed. G. Kittel, VOL. III, Stuttgart 1927-29, p. 241f.

"Synoptic perspective"; we do acknowledge that the sentence certainly applies to Luke's Gospel. Mark consistently contradicts it where there is a reference to cultic matters, but what about Matthew? Are there not in Matthew's Gospel indications of some measure of acceptance of Temple and cult? We do indeed frequently find expressions such as "the house of God," "the holy city," and others. But surely these represent merely the traditional language of reverence which Jesus or the Evangelist has used almost accidentally; they tell us nothing about approval or rejection of the things mentioned. Moreover the New Testament speaks blandly of the Jewish Temple as the ἱερόν, the word which the Septuagint solemnly avoided in order to distinguish God's holy place in Jerusalem from the host of pagan temples, ἱερά, scattered throughout the ancient world. Again a word from the Sermon on the Mount might seem to suggest an indirect approval of sacrifice:

If you are offering your gift at the altar, and there remember that your brother has something against you, leave your gift there before the altar and go; first be reconciled to your brother, and then come and offer your gift. (Mt. v.23-24)

If it is more important to be reconciled to your brother—the offender or the offended, both are possible—then is reconciliation not involved in sacrifice? And yet to ask that question is to miss the main point of the utterance; that even the slightest difference with a brother—and it must be slight, if one "remembers" it—is important enough to cancel out the holiness of the hour for sacrifice. This sacrifice is chosen merely as an example of the holiest obligations of the relationship between man and God. The words of the text do not refer to the regulations of the Jerusalem cult, for there in fact no lay person offers a sacrifice but only a priest; and even presupposing this priestly mediation the word would still be strange and inappropriate, for it could apply only to a Jerusalemite, hardly to a Galilean (but it is to a Galilean that according to Matthew the word is addressed) and could not therefore claim to be in any way an unconditional command. Jesus is not speaking of any existing cultic regulation, He is selecting something from the Old Testament, which often speaks of the layman's sacrifice on the altar—the story of Cain and Abel comes immediately to mind—to illustrate holiness at its greatest and setting right relations with one's brother over against it as a holier duty. There is therefore here no indirect sanctioning of the cultic demands; on the contrary it is a general and unconditional statement that where a man denies his brother reconciliation he cannot please God, and where a man asks his brother for reconciliation only then does he make a proper sacrifice. From this conscious disregard of current cultic usage one might argue for a fundamental remoteness in Jesus' connexion with it rather than the reverse.

Thus this word from the Sermon on the Mount does not amount to a "Yes" to Temple and sacrifice from Jesus' lips. The effect of "No" to everything cultic in Mark's Gospel is indeed heightened by it. We are concerned, however, not only with the question whether the cult can withstand the shock of Jesus' Gospel—and in fact that question is not really solved by the "No" once uttered in history—but also with the question whether the Gospel makes any positive reference in its own profundity to questions concerning cult—and now we mean not the Jewish cult but "eschatological" cult. It is to this problem that we must now turn our attention, before we can finally survey the question of cult and Gospel as a whole.

III. THE GOSPEL ON CULT

WE have uncovered a wealth of material, and numerous points have emerged which throw light on our problem of Gospel and cult from very many angles, but for all that we have really only learned how the Jewish cult is viewed and judged from the Gospel's point of view. We have found rejection of the Jewish cult in the Gospels, sometimes restrained, sometimes blunt; but nowhere have we found cult itself challenged or impugned. The Gospel itself speaks of forgiveness and sanctification, of sin and sacrifice, of cleanness and uncleanness. The idea of cult is very much alive in the Gospel, and how could it be otherwise when there is no faith without cult nor ever can be? Our immediate task therefore must be to determine upon what cultic basis Jesus' Gospel takes its stand, and to what cultic goal it leads. So far we have seen the Jewish cult at the bar of the Gospel, now we enquire about the Gospel in the light of cult.

In doing this we have also to reckon with another and related point. So far our attention has been directed to the record of Jesus' works for an assessment of His attitude to the cultic usages of His time, but if we are going to find out how the cult idea has influenced and coloured the Gospel, then it is familiar and unforgettable words from the Gospels which immediately spring to mind. And whereas we have had to remember that the accounts of Jesus' works reflected to a greater or lesser degree the characteristic attitude of the reporting community, here, where we are dealing with words, we may at least presume to be getting closer to Jesus' own point of view. This new bit of work therefore complements what we have done critically as well as materially. Since, however, it would be a very considerable task and little to our purpose to examine every individual utterance for its cultic content or colouring, we shall rather select certain elements basic to Jesus' preaching and indicate their particular cultic significance.

First and almost as a matter of course there is the concept of the Kingdom of God or the Kingdom of Heaven. I say Kingdom of God not kingship of God, for, whatever the Aramaic may mean, the Greek word undoubtedly signifies something in space and time and not merely a divine function. That is clear from the phraseology of many sayings. We read, for example, that one enters the Kingdom of God or is thrown out "into outer darkness," that one shuts it up, that the keys of the Kingdom of Heaven will be given to Peter. One sits or reclines at table in this Kingdom of God, there is eating and drinking in it. All these expressions make it clear that the Kingdom of Heaven is the House or the City of God. In the same way there stands over against it the house or city of Satan. When Jesus retorts to the charge that He casts out demons by Beelzebub, He shows the foolishness of the charge by means of an illustration: "if a house is divided against itself that house will not be able to stand" (Mk. III.25). Beelzebub is also called the master of a house and the demons members of his household (Mt. x.25). There is therefore a house of God and a house of Satan, gates through which one enters the Kingdom of Heaven and life, and gates of Hell which do not prevail over the holy rock though Satan and his demonic hosts attempt incessantly to break into the "strong man's house." There are further variations of the metaphor—the father, the head of the household, guests invited to the royal palace, servants who wait; they occur regularly throughout the whole range of Jesus' sayings and there is none that does not have carefully considered significance.

Admittedly the house metaphor is capable of many different usages and meanings. Jesus himself speaks of the house of David or the house of Israel, and means the group dwelling in a certain place and conscious that it is in a certain line of descent. There is no real analogy, however, between the phrase House of God or City of God and those others referring to history or to the nation: the analogy is too unequivocal—it is with the Temple, which is called His holy house, or the city which is called the "city of the great king." And were there any doubt about this another fact would remove it and confirm what we have said. No contemporary or later Rabbinic text speaks of "entering the kingdom of heaven"; analogies for such a way of speaking are to be found in the historical entry into

the holy land, in pilgrimages to the holy city and in festive
entrances into the holy Temple. So in Ps. cxviii.19f. we read:

> Open to me the gates of righteousness,
>> that I may enter through them and give thanks to the Lord.
> This is the gate of the Lord;
>> the righteous shall enter through it.

Or there is the complaint of Lam. 1.10: Jerusalem

> . . . has seen the nations invade her sanctuary,
>> those whom thou didst forbid to enter thy congregation.

Mowinckel has therefore spoken of cultic entrance-regula-
tions (*thoroth d'entrée*) which were observed in the Temple's
festival liturgies and which are the Old Testament background
for Jesus' sayings about entering the Kingdom of God. Thus
this *basileia* of God's is taking up its own particular position over
against the house or city which God once chose as His dwelling.
This confrontation is all the more instructive when we consider
closely connected ideas on both sides. For example the Temple
in Jerusalem is the place of God's kingship; His throne is there,
as everyone knows who has read the story of the call of Isaiah;
the festival of His enthronement was celebrated there, issuing
in the hope of God's eschatological dominion. On the other
hand this *basileia* of which Jesus speaks is inseparably fused with
apocalyptic ideas of God's coming world—the "Olam habbah."
The idea is the exact eschatological counterpart of the earlier
mentioned Jewish belief that the Temple and city of Jerusalem
were the sacred centre of the earth and would one day attract
all peoples. This aspect gives to the familiar and somewhat
restricted house metaphor the heavenly dimension of infinity
proper to God's world. What is nearest and ordinary comprises what is far distant and immeasurable. Nevertheless in
spite of this unspeakable range that is involved the house
metaphor is carefully retained, as we know from the well-known
words (Mt. viii.11f.):

Many will come from east and west and sit at table with Abraham, Isaac,
and Jacob in the kingdom of heaven, while the sons of the kingdom will be
thrown into the outer darkness.

The second half of the saying is based on the familiar picture of the brightly-lit home from which children are driven into the darkness of night. And on this house—according to the first half—the peoples of the whole earth, the "many" will converge, an innumerable company of God's invited guests.

One will perhaps object that to represent God's Kingdom as God's House or God's City is merely a pretty metaphor, a manner of speaking. What has the Temple at Jerusalem to do with the actual Kingdom of God? It is certainly "merely" a metaphor, but a metaphor with a distinctly eschatological character. The fact is that, where we are dealing with an eschatological message, metaphor and parable are necessarily the media of proclamation. No doubt this is an attempt to make comprehensible the incomprehensible riches of God's world to come, but the comprehensible image is required as a mirror into which believing eyes can look in order to see the in-comprehensible. No image is arbitrary, the "house of God" metaphor is not someone's meaningless whim, it really does convey to human understanding the eschatological fact of the Kingdom of God, veiling it or unveiling it according to one's point of view. It highlights the cultic foundation on which this *basileia* stands. And now we must ask, what is this foundation?

In the Old Testament the Temple has a threefold function; it is the house where God rules, where He judges, and where one worships Him. No one will contest the close connexion between this threefold function and the characteristic function of God's *basileia*. The idea of kingly rule is already implicit in the word *basileia*, and judgment is an inalienable part of Jesus' message. But wherever this kingly and judicial action of God is mentioned the local metaphor is always also employed. Some are to be "cast out," others are to be invited to "enter into the joy" of their master, or as an old saying from the Fourth Gospel has it: "In my Father's house are many rooms." And the distinction between Temple and *basileia* is of course per-fectly clear. Jesus knows and says little of God's constant holy presence in the Temple—the saying in the story of the Cleansing of the Temple: "you shall not make my Father's house a house of trade" (Jn. II.16) is one of the few that might be quoted. This presence is suspended and given an infinite renewal in: "the kingdom of God is at hand." It is distinct from all titles and reasons which one might seek and honour in the here and now. This being at hand which is predicated of God's Kingdom and House is a "new" eschatological event. In the Jewish cult God's House is the place where He operates His *basileia* and will operate it; here it is the product of His rule. There the *basileia* is connected with a definite place and is conditioned by all the historical circumstances of the people and of the land. Here the *basileia* is the eternal place of God's abiding with His own, and in face of its eschatological glory all historical limits take flight. This very contrast, however, clearly reveals the close connexion between the cultic sanctuary and the eschatological House of God.

What are we to say now about what one might call the most important of all functions of the Jewish Temple, the priestly function, which raised the Temple to the status of a place of unending worship? Where are the faithful of the end-time or even Jesus' disciples ever called priests? It is a fact that in the Gospels the eschatological *basileia* is never called the place of eternal priestly worship. And for other and more profound reasons the priestly function is absent. How, one may ask, can there be priests, i.e. mediators between God and men, in God's eschatological House and Kingdom? This is the place characterised by that immediacy in virtue of which one can "see God" and the elect are even called "sons of God"; all the poor and oppressed and sinners are invited into this holy House. A new and unheard-of thing takes the place of priestly service; the Master's disciples and the peoples of the earth will eat with Him in His father's Kingdom. This is the holy and eternal fact which puts an end to all priestly functions. Indeed the contrast is so decisive and important that we must look for new words and ideas to express it.

The idea of *ekklesia* is closely connected with that of *basileia* and is of course inherited from the Old Testament. And as in the Old Testament Temple and community belong together— they are indeed interchangeable, as we see from the earlier quoted text from Lam. 1.10—so also the cultic background is visible wherever Jesus speaks of His *ekklesia*. It is the word for the community assembled before their God for celebration and worship, i.e. assembled in the Temple. Jesus does not in fact speak often of the *ekklesia*, but in one important passage, in the address to Peter, cultic motifs emerge clearly and undisguisedly:

On this rock I will build my church and the gates of Hades shall not prevail against it. (Mt. xvi.18, note)

What can have inspired this metaphor if not the sight of the Jewish Temple towering above the deep valley of Hinnom, the Jewish Hell, on the holy rock? The word "build" which occurs here is used a second time in the well-known saying (Mk. xiv.58):

I will build another [temple].

The eschatological community is therefore a Temple which the Master will erect. The difference is striking and profound: in Jerusalem a Temple which is a building of stone embellished with the costliest materials the earth can boast, here the temple of which Jesus speaks, something as built up of men, burdened with all the earth's cares and infirmities; in Jerusalem a ceaseless sacrifice of animals on holy altars, here a meal shared with the Master "in His Father's kingdom"; in Jerusalem in all divine service the exercise of ecclesiastical authority over men, here the Master Himself in the midst of His own "as one who serves" (Lk. xxii.27). Nor should one be surprised that God's *basileia* and the Master's *ekklesia* share the same metaphor. Already in the Old Testament the close relationship between the two is adumbrated and certainly here they belong together even more closely. *Basileia* means from God's point of view that which the word *ekklesia* describes from the Master's point of view. In view of this relationship the temple metaphor becomes the point of coincidence which reveals their essential identity. Those that are oppressed with care and want, poverty and guilt, whom the Master calls to Himself, are of the Kingdom of God. And because He calls them to His Father's holy House, He builds the temple where God reigns eternally, and destroys the other, which formerly presumed to be the place of God's kingly rule.

This is given the clearest possible expression in yet another of Jesus' sayings, the original form of which is probably:

I will destroy this temple and in three days I will build another.
(Mk. xiv.58)

This is in the first instance an eschatological prophecy of disaster closely related to a later Jewish intimation:

> The building of Zion shall be shaken in order that it may again be built.

One finds this prophecy in the Apocalypse of Baruch (XXXII.2) and similar prophecies in II Esdras (VII.26, XIII.36). Clearly and urgently Jesus is announcing the early destruction of the Temple; perhaps too His words represent an expression of the popular expectation that at the end-time Solomon's Temple would be destroyed and replaced in a tremendous and miraculous rebuilding either of the sanctuary alone or of the entire holy city. Nevertheless one thing is certain, that here it is not a question of darkly hinting at an approaching event the time and manner of the coming of which no one knows. Here the destruction of the Temple is Jesus' task and avowed intention. No doubt the meaning of the prophecy is necessarily also eschatological; be that as it may this destruction is to be the Master's unconditional and historical act. Implicit in Jesus' words is the knowledge that now the time of God's eschatological action is beginning and that the Master is called and empowered to implement this eschatological scheme. It is the same knowledge as is implicit in another way in the cleansing of the Temple, knowledge of a summons to battle against the Jewish Temple in view of the imminence of eschatological fulfilment. This battle is also conceived as both the historical and eschatological task and privilege of the Son of Man. The saying illumines as with a sudden shaft of bright light the many veiled and open attacks on individual aspects of the cult which we observed earlier in the Gospel tradition, and shows that they represent a consistent and basic direction of all Jesus' works and proclamation. No prescribed ritual can any longer promise purity. No sacrifice can blot out sins, no holy Sabbath laws are any longer valid, priests are His Father's enemies, the wicked husbandmen of God's vineyard. He might have said: "I am come to destroy the Temple," an apocryphal saying has it: "I am come to destroy sacrifice" (Gosp. of the Ebion. Fr.11).

The second half of the saying concerning the Temple is perhaps even more important. What is meant by "another temple"? The Fourth Evangelist (II.19) with superb partiality refers the saying to Jesus' death and resurrection. It is his own late interpretation: he has suppressed the original word "another" and chosen to understand the Resurrection as the Risen Jesus' own act, whereas for earliest Christianity the fact that "He was raised" is an indisputable element of the faith. To Jewish minds this "otherness" of the new Temple suggested an almost unspeakably celestial kind of Temple, the costly splendour of which is celebrated in fantastic pictures. These were of course known to the early Christian community and magnificently portrayed in the Johannine Apocalypse, but here an ancient and profound understanding of these pictures is preserved. It is taken for granted that God will be in and with His holy people. The "other temple" which the Master will build is therefore the eschatological community of His disciples for, as we saw, the phrase "I will build" occurs again only in the word to Peter and there it has for object "my church."

Kingdom of God and church are therefore linked together in the "House of God" metaphor, and become one with it over against the present and in anticipation of the future "other temple." But who has a place in this new and different House of God? According to Jewish cultic regulations only those are admitted who are born Jews, obey God's holy Law, and whose sins are expiated by holy sacrifice. The Gospel according to St Matthew paints a very different picture when it describes the eschatological community which gathers around Jesus in the ancient and now newly cleansed courts of the Temple, cleansed by His driving forth of the money-changers and merchants. Now the people who have a place in the Temple are the blind and the lame whom He healed and the children chanting: "Hosanna to the son of David!" And this emphasis that becomes so evident shortly before Jesus' death is found at all the milestones of His ministry. Before and after the Sermon on the Mount this company of the needy and sinners emerges— they are the eschatologically bidden guests—before the choosing and sending forth of the twelve disciples, before the miraculous feeding of the multitude. Perhaps the emphasis on this particular aspect of Jesus' story is peculiar to Matthew, but there are words and parables enough and to spare to assure us that it really was a basic factor in His ministry:

Those who are well have no need of a physician, but those who are sick; I came not to call the righteous, but sinners. (Mk. ii.17)

or:

I was sent only to the lost sheep of the house of Israel.
(Mt. xv.24)

This is the burden of the beatitudes and of the parable of the royal Marriage Feast from which the invited guests exclude themselves and to which beggars and cripples from the hedges and byways are summoned. And when one asks what is the point of this election of the dispossessed and repudiated of society one should remember that when Jesus had ended His Sermon on the Mount He healed, according to Matthew, a leper, a heathen, and an old woman one after the other. They are people strictly excluded by cultic law from all worship, or suffered only in exceptional circumstances. They are representative of a larger company—the sick and weak, those possessed of devils and the unclean, the poor and the beggar class, who could not pay the tax for Temple and sacrifice, above all the "publicans and sinners." It would seem that the only explanation of the common currency of this phrase, combining men following proscribed occupations and those who transgress the sacred law, is to be found in their common failure in cultic purity. It is, however, in company with such men that Christ allows Himself to be entertained: all the barriers erected by an exclusive cult are down, and the immediacy of the Master's relationship with the lost sanctifies them more effectively than the mediation of the cult sanctifies the righteous. The supreme representation of this anti-cult tendency, which is the eschatological "divine plan," is therefore the parable of the Prodigal Son. He leaves his father's house, keeps company with the basest and uncleanest characters, and when he returns as a beggar his father takes him to his heart in unstinted love:

This my son was dead, and is alive again; he was lost, and is found.
(Lk. xv.24)

It might still seem that the conflict between Jewish cult and Jesus' eschatological outlook was too general to be of much consequence, and that other motives may have been present (we shall come to this later) if there were not indications in plenty that the conflict was sharp and relentless, one that was to be fought out to the death. The three most basic elements of the Jewish cult undergo in Jesus' preaching a profound change. According to Jewish cultic law one must first of all be of pure Jewish extraction before one can take part in sacrifice, but in Jesus' doctrine we read: "Many—and that means, as we know, those also of heathen and Gentile birth— will come from east and west and sit at table with Abraham, Isaac, and Jacob in the kingdom of heaven, while the sons of the kingdom will be thrown into the outer darkness." In such words and in corresponding works the stipulation about birth is simply ignored. In other places it is restated completely and with astounding novelty, e.g. in the blessing of the children. Jesus not only admits to the House and Kingdom of God those who had to wait outside the doors of the Jewish Temple, He also exalts that section of society which has neither adult age nor adult understanding to the status of exemplary "children of the kingdom," to the blessed status of recipients of eschatological revelation. And whereas in the cult the saying runs that through expiatory sacrifice Israel becomes pure as a child here on the contrary we find: "unless you turn and become like little children." In the one instance being born of the seed of Abraham opens the door to the sanctuary; in the other being born from above, being converted, unlocks the doors of the Kingdom of God. This contrast is important for the understanding of Jesus' attitude to cultic regulations, because it shows how He gives to every natural birth the hallowing which Judaism accorded under the strictest conditions to Jewish birth. Jesus sees also in natural birth the image of that eschatological birth which consecrates every man for entrance into the coming kingdom. The eschatological fulfilment of human life goes back to the natural beginning.

Jesus' attitude to the second basic element, the sacred Law, is even more revealing. The problem is so great and so complex that I refer only to those aspects of it which concern cultic matters. For Jesus the Torah was not only the inviolable norm of all action; it was also the inalienable basis of His preaching. It was both of these things to such a degree that large parts of the Sermon on the Mount are simply interpretations of the second

F

tablet of the Decalogue. And yet this Law also stands under the shadow of the old order and passes away before the light of the Gospel as "heaven and earth will pass away" (Mk. XIII.31). We see already a sign of this passing away in the fact that no cultic regulation is ever acknowledged in Jesus' message, and that those that are mentioned here and there are actually contradicted. Everything which sanctifies in a ritual sense is swept away, swept away so ruthlessly that even special cultic ordinances like prayer and fasting lose their ancient sanctifying significance. If prayer in public places is mere idle prattle, then obviously it means that a severe blow is dealt at the holy ordinances which embrace every pious Jew, and a person's private room has become a holier place than the Temple. If there is to be no more fasting before men, then the rules preparing the individual for the fast go by the board and the traditional sanctity of festivals is altogether lost. Behind all these revolutionary attitudes is the more profound idea of the eschatological community which will be founded when God's Kingdom comes, when the Father's House appears, in which the individual is set free from the atomised and divided existence to which the fulfilment of the old cultic ordinances committed him and is led into the fellowship of those who will eat and drink with Him in His Father's House, in His Father's Kingdom.

It is never openly stated that Jesus' Gospel has eliminated cultic commandments from the body of Old Testament law: it simply happens. Sabbath observance and handwashing, rules concerning taxes and purity simply don't count. A silent step, tremendous in its silence, is taken from cultic constraint into the freedom of moral action. There is one other indication of how this step was taken. Jesus speaks of the "law and the prophets" as the indestructible (and certainly undestroyed by Him) norms of human life. But there never was a time when a Jew could ascribe the same canonical validity to the prophets as to the Law of Moses. The only norm comparable in holiness (perhaps it was higher) with the Law was the cult practised in the Temple at Jerusalem. What Jesus did was to replace the cult by the prophets, and to treat them not as mere interpreters of the Law as the Jews had done, but as themselves bearers of the word of God in their own right. For all the diversity of their voices they blend into one in proclaiming and demanding as Jesus also proclaims and demands: "You shall love the Lord your God . . . you shall love your neighbour as yourself. On these two commandments depend all the law and the prophets" (Mt. xxii.40). Mark deliberately adds: "to love him with all the heart, and with all the understanding, and with all the strength, and to love one's neighbour as oneself, is much more than all whole burnt offerings and sacrifices" (xii.33). The battle against the cult was of course waged by the prophets themselves in earlier days, and it is not accidental that in this struggle, new and yet so very old, Jesus often quotes the prophets' words: "I desire mercy and not sacrifice" (Mt. ix.13); "My house shall be called a house of prayer . . . but you have made it a den of robbers."

At this point another important matter calls for consideration. The duality (Law and cult) of this divinely-ordained foundation of the proudly pure life of the nation is also its weakness. However one may interpret the duality, whether with a priestly emphasis so that the Law is thought to conform to the cult or with the Pharisaic emphasis so that the cult is thought to be based on the Law, the necessity remains of regarding as the consistent will of God what expresses itself in disparate and manifold cultic and moral directives, not to speak of Laws in the justiciary sense. The particular sanctity of a sacrifical law and the general validity of the commandment about loving have this in common—they are God's will, they have been handed down. For the believing Jew, therefore, there can be no setting aside of the cultic regulations without destroying the completeness of the Torah. Similarly and for the same reason there can be no question of asking what is the greatest commandment, or of answering that the whole of the Law and the prophets is contained in the commandment about love. To do so is to set oneself up as a judge of the will of God. In Jesus' Gospel the cultic prescriptions have disappeared, and the way is open to comprehend the remaining moral commandments in one basic commandment. Now not only can one ask what the first commandment is, one must ask. The sacred mediation of cult no longer exists. Whether in the company of his neighbours or in the privacy of his own room a man now stands immediately before the face of the heavenly Father, who sees into the inmost recesses of his heart. The ancient cult is destroyed and from its ruins there blossoms the flower of a new life of holy love for God and for one's neighbour.

But now if the mediation of the cult is gone it means also that the way is gone which leads the individual believer to the ultimate and holiest goal of fellowship with God. The Gospel now indicates what the way is and what the goal. One might ask whether the goal is after all any different? Let us look at only two passages which show the influence of cultic ideas on the Gospel goal. The first is the well-known beatitude (Mt. v.8):

> Blessed are the pure in heart, for they shall see God.

Both the idea of purity and the promise concerning "seeing God" are cultic, but the term "the pure in heart" also indicates the contrast of inner integrity to that cleanness from spot and blemish afforded by sacrifice and cultic observances. There is an affinity here not only with the Psalms and Jewish wisdom literature but also with Roman and Hellenistic sources. When the "pure heart" is spoken of, it does not mean the making of a distinction between the action and the heart (the motive)— the New Testament does not make that distinction; the "pure heart" is a reference to that unity and consistency in which the act mirrors the heart and the heart inspires the act, in other words that holiness which is God's nature and His gift to His own. Here, however, we have an explanation which takes us far beyond all cultic superficiality to that context in which the heart becomes the place where God dwells in greater purity and sanctity than in any temple on earth. The promise that the pure in heart will "see God" goes even farther. It is in fact an old Jewish expectation and an element of the salvation which the cult mediates. It indicates that unthinkable miracle of God's becoming visible to men, the Invisible and Hidden One, dwelling in an unapproachable light, and preserves in the very immediacy of this face-to-face meeting the awful and inevitable "distance" of this seeing. There grows up therefore a connexion between the hidden things of the pure heart, which are never native but always God's gift, and the hidden things of God which can never be seen or fathomed. In "seeing God" man is given access in visible fullness to what humanly speaking is the invisibility of God, and the veil of all priestly or cultic mediation which formerly guaranteed such a seeing falls to the ground.

If this first text we have examined suggests more strongly the reaction of the Gospel against the cult, the next one undoubtedly indicates a real measure of ultimate agreement:

You, therefore, must be perfect, as your heavenly Father is perfect.
(Mt. v.48)

This bears a close resemblance to the Old Testament injunction that applied equally to the individual and to the nation as a whole:

You shall be holy; for I the Lord your God am holy.
(Lev. xix.2)

The saying, which is frequently repeated, appears also in another form:

You shall be blameless before the Lord your God.
(Deut. xviii.13)

That which is the fulfilment of all God's acts in the history of this people, that which was the ultimate and most profound reality of this holy cult, is in fact the aim and meaning and eschatological reality of the Gospel. It is therefore at once the new and the old word of God, at once the new and the old divine reality. It therefore conquers the cult, which remains always a provisional thing, however much of the beauty of holiness it may contain, in terms of a final eschatological "fulfilment" given it in view of the coming Kingdom and House of God.

There remains the question: does the Gospel overcome and "fulfil" the ultimate and holiest element of the cult: sacrifice? According to Matthew's Gospel Jesus twice quotes Hosea; "I desire steadfast love and not sacrifice." Also this express rejection of sacrifice would seem to be confirmed by the fact that we nowhere in the Gospels hear of Jesus taking part in the daily sacrifice or indeed in any cultic observances. It is not difficult to see the reason for this abstention which to a pious Jew would be sinful. The saying: "My house shall be a house of prayer" looks far beyond all cultic sacrifices to one true function of God's holy house, that of prayer "for all nations."

Jesus' use of the Hosea text is also the introduction into the Gospel of a basic prophetic argument, that it is not sacrifice which expiates but steadfast love for one's needy neighbour; that it is not the pious contrivance which sanctifies, be it ever so worthy and ever so godly, but the loving heart. Sacrifice therefore loses its particular grace and point and its power to bestow holiness from one particular place over individuals and the nation, and instead wherever loving hearts beat there is found the foundation of holiness which reconciles the oppressed soul with his neighbour and with his God. If this Old Testament saying be not explicit enough, then surely the fifth petition of the Lord's Prayer is, or Jesus' teaching delivered to His disciples in the parable of the Wicked Servant —that the duty and the power of forgiving love is immeasurable. Indeed on the basis of this and other such sayings one feels bound to say that in the Gospels this love is the holiness and creates the holiness which was the aim of sacrifice. It is for that reason that the Scribe can say that to love God and to love one's neighbour as oneself is much more than all whole burnt offerings and sacrifices, and Jesus can reply: "You are not far from the kingdom of God." It is also for that reason that the old and yet new saying in the Sermon on the Mount, "you must be perfect" can appear in Luke in the form:

Be merciful, even as your Father is merciful.

(Lk. vi.36)

The merciful, loving heart is more sacred and more sanctifying than the altar.

This might mean, however, that only one function of sacrifice was abandoned, that which gave the individual access to God, and that the question of the validity of sacrifice in other respects, e.g. as God's means of binding Himself and His people together in a sacred fellowship, was still undecided. In fact there can be no doubt that this, the greatest virtue of sacrifice, is also gone. Do we not read that "the sons of the kingdom will be thrown into the outer darkness," and that the Gentiles are to be gathered with the patriarchs in a new and everlasting community? What all this is saying is in effect that the coming of the Kingdom of God and the incipient building of the "other" temple, the eschatological community of God, deprives both Temple and sacrifice of all power and holiness. When God reigns in His Kingdom and rules His House with fatherly carefulness, He with His people, and His people with Him, then in the fullness of this fellowship there is no place for sacrifice. One might of course object that what has happened is simply that an ancient Jewish idea concerning the end of all sacrifice at the end-time has been taken over concretely into the gospel of the Kingdom of God, and ask whether one can really call that the overthrow and fulfilment of sacrifice. Are we not still talking about hope for the inconceivable future, for what is coming upon the earth? But this Kingdom of God, this House of God, not only is coming; it also is present and operative. Through every sign and suggestion of its presence the brightness of the eschatological fulfilment will stream, and in such brightness the sacrificial flame will go out. We shall take notice of only a few of these signs, which are important in this context.

First we shall speak of Jesus' miracles of healing. In Jesus' day Jews believed, as they did in the Old Testament, that illness and misfortune were punishment for the sins of the nation or of the individual. They showed that God had turned away His face from them, and ultimately only the God-given power of penance and sacrifice could propitiate His wrath. And yet illness and need continued to oppress the holy land and the children of God as before, defying the sanctity accorded by God to sacrifice and worship in His honour. Here, however, in Jesus' ministry, by an amazing power of healing—"the finger of God," all illness is cured:

The blind receive their sight and the lame walk, lepers are cleansed and the deaf hear, and the dead are raised up, and the poor have good news preached to them. (Mt. xi.5)

Now therefore it really is true:

Blessed are those who mourn, for they shall be comforted.
                                                        (Mt. v.4)

Now there is taking place as a visible sign of the proximity of the Kingdom of God what the pious in the cult had hoped for, and what the maker of sacrifices had regarded as the divine enigma. God's Kingdom and His House are now the true

home, the place of freedom and relief for those bowed down by
need and suffering.

The driving out of demons is also worthy of particular
attention. Mark's Gospel sees this as the distinctive indication
of the eschatological event, and Jesus Himself confirms it in
the saying:

If it is with the finger of God that I cast out demons, then the kingdom
of God has come upon you. (Lk. xi.20)

The casting out of demons was not unfamiliar to the Jewish
cult. Indeed it was an essential part of the great festival on the
Day of Atonement. The whole point of the ceremony was to
banish demons and all sins into that sinister and unholy place
beyond the habitations of Jewry, the wilderness, in order that
land and people should be holy as on the day of creation.
Following hard and impressively upon this solemnity came the
Festival of Atonement. Now, however, the demons are driven
out and "destroyed" by the silent power of Him who is the
Holy One of God. Even death is helpless in face of this power,
as we learn from several famous narratives, and in virtue of it
the Master can actually say: "your sins are forgiven." In the
Jewish cult sickness and need, sin and death are the inexplicable
contradiction of the salvation and sanctity which sacrifice,
instituted by God, was able to accord, reminding one of the
darkness that enshrouds all human life and all history, which
also encompasses the sacrificial flame and is not illumined by
it, and driving one for comfort to the expectation of that time
of fulfilment when "death shall be no more, neither shall there
be mourning nor crying nor pain any more" (Rev. xxi.4).
Now, however, it is like mist that scatters in the morning light
of the Kingdom of God.

Again one should recall the choosing of the disciples who
accompanied the Master until His death. Their relationship
to Him was not a student-master relationship such as the
rabbis knew. They were called to discipleship by a word of
power, by Jesus' transforming word—of which transformation
the new names Peter and Boanerges are token; and similarly
it was in virtue of this eschatological power that the promise
was made to them:

You . . . will . . . sit on twelve thrones, judging the twelve tribes of
Israel. (Mk. xix.28; Lk. xxii.30)

Even in the mean and difficult days of their discipleship the joy and fullness of the eschatological day is in them and around them:

> Can the wedding guests fast while the bridegroom is with them?
> (Mk. II.19)

And Peter received the promise:

> I will give you the keys of the kingdom of heaven, and whatever you bind on earth shall be bound in heaven, and whatever you loose on earth, shall be loosed in heaven.   (Mt. XVI.19)

But "binding" and "loosing," properly understood, are cultic functions, indeed they are priestly functions.   That little group of disciples becomes in the here and now the kernel, the first nucleus of the holy eschatological community of the Kingdom of God.

Leaving aside for the moment the sign from heaven at Jesus' baptism, we would claim attention for something more important than all the foregoing, something which permeates the whole Gospel tradition of Jesus' words and work and presents the mysterious eschatological counterpart to Jewish sacrifice. Three years ago in Sweden I had an opportunity of speaking on the meaning and significance of the early Christian custom of sharing a common meal. My lecture was published in the American *Journal of Biblical Literature*, 1937. A briefer statement here will therefore suffice. The custom is connected with the eschatological expectation of an eschatological feast and with the eating and drinking habits of pious Jews; it conjoins eschatological fulfilment and everyday practice in a new unity replete with eschatological significance. Jesus eats not only with His disciples, but also with Pharisees and publicans, with righteous men and sinners, with high and low. Indeed this was so essential a part of the Master's work and witness that the people actually said of Him maliciously:

> Behold a glutton and a drunkard, a friend of tax-collectors and sinners.
> (Mt. XI.19)

The gospel of the Kingdom is so full of sayings concerning meals, eating and drinking, hungering and thirsting, that there is not *one* element of it which is not expressed somewhere in terms of a meal-metaphor. The blessing of this Gospel message, the challenge, the commandment, the promise, all are comprehended in this meal context and in the corresponding custom. He is the bridegroom celebrating the wedding feast, the Son of Man who eats and drinks, the father who gives bread to his children, even His healing of those possessed of devils is described in terms of feeding the children (Mk. vii.27). This meal is both metaphor and reality, both parable and event; it reveals in the word what the act adumbrates, and sets forth in the act what the word by implication promises. Here we have the centre, around which all Jesus' words and work revolve and in virtue of which they have unity. The meal takes place here and now, and yet remains in the nature of an eschatological message. The mystery of the meal explains the present and uncovers the coming fulfilment. In it there is brought together and interwoven all that the existence and the coming of the Kingdom of God involve. One can scarcely overlook what is at once a radical contrast and an essential relatedness between this meal instituted by Jesus and the Jewish ceremony of sacrifice. On the one hand in the Temple we have a strictly regulated cult operated for the benefit of Israel by a sacred priestly order according to sacred tradition and by divine commission. On the other hand in the Christian festival we have first of all no holy house, but instead wherever men eat is holy ground. In the Christian festival there is no tradition and no commission other than that of a father in his own house giving thanks to his heavenly Father as the giver of food and drink. In the Christian festival there are no priests at work, no congregation, expectant in reverent stillness, but poor and hungry folk satisfying themselves at a simple meal. And yet here Jesus who distributes and blesses effects a deeper and truer holiness than the holiest sacrifice ever effected, for here we have something like a dark and early sign of a fulfilment dreamed of and long-hoped for; here we have, revealing itself under the semblances of a present fellowship so poor and mean, the holy power of the final and perfect Kingdom of God. And of course one understands now why the Kingdom of God is represented as a house and a city. In this heavenly home and this heavenly city the nations of the earth and the poor will come "and sit at table with Abraham, Isaac, and Jacob."

The real eschatological nature of the communal meal and

its eschatological festivity is borne out clearly in three examples. The first is Jesus' eating and drinking with "publicans and sinners." The true significance of this meal lies not only in Jesus' pulling down of the barriers which Jewish cult had raised against all unholy enemies of the people and their faith, nor only in His consciousness of being sent to the lost sheep of the house of Israel for whom no flame burned on the Temple altars. It also and above all lies in the fact that here in this fellowship, which was not a fellowship of holy priest with holy people but of "the Holy One of God" with "sinners," we have a sign of the "eating and drinking" which there will be in God's House. This is therefore two things, an ordinary meal and an eschatological feast. The miraculous feeding of the people by the Sea of Galilee is an even clearer illustration. This too is a simple ordinary meal eaten on a spring evening as the sun sinks over the lake. Jesus is the host and entertains His guests exactly as the father of a Jewish family would, observing pious customs and sharing simple food. He also feeds them, however, by means of a miracle which at once reveals and veils the power and stature of the Son of Man. The very ordinariness which Jesus used the miracle to achieve makes it an even more impressive sign of an eschatological meal which (behind the veil of the passing present) unites the Lord and His people. And here for the first time new cultic gestures and forms emerge. The disciples move back and forward between the standing figure of the Master—He said prayers over the bread and the fish—and those sitting around on the grass; they receive the broken pieces of bread from His hands and offer them to each individual. It is a "service"—the Master was amongst His disciples as "one who serves" (Lk. xxii.27). As if to emphasise this atmosphere of holy cultic solemnity Mark and Matthew tell us—and the words are almost exclusive to these passages—that Jesus "sent away" the crowd when they had eaten. It is of course the prerogative of the priest who has completed his sacred liturgy to "send away" (cf. Num. vi.27; Ecclesiasticus l.20f.; Lk. i.22) the people who stand watching and waiting. Here therefore we have an eschatological cult in embryo, if we may so express it; it is a quite special thing as the other cult was also special, but its speciality is not the speciality of an historical origin but of an eschatological goal.

It is not distinguished by its form from all so-called profane action as sacrifice was; it is in fact the ordinary daily customs of poor and pious men which constitute its form. Its content flows from the person of the Master to the company assembled around Him. In His life, in His very existence there lies still hidden and yet in the miracle, revealed, the glory and holiness of the eschatological Kingdom of God; and this is the essence of that glory and holiness—a meal that is the Lord's meal and a brotherly eating together and a love-feast.

The meal celebrated with the disciples on the eve of Jesus' death follows the pattern of the miraculous feeding of the crowds and of common usage. Here again Jesus is the father of the family giving bread to eat and wine to drink to His own. His disciples are His relatives or His guests, perhaps also from now on the heirs of His meal. They no longer wait at table, they are waited upon; and the person who waits upon them is— according to Luke's account, which is certainly not contradicted by Matthew and Mark—Jesus Himself. He is not only the Lord, He is also the One who serves. There is one obvious difference, however, and that is the clearly expressed liturgical solemnity that permeates Jesus' words and gestures on this occasion, for—quite apart from whether this last meal was a Passover meal or not—certainly *in the course of it* Jesus speaks words and performs acts which according to Jewish custom fell to the father of the house at the beginning of a communal meal, and definitely mark them out, therefore, as cultic. Whereas the significance of all previous meals has been implicit or embodied in the Master, on this occasion the word spoken over the cup points far beyond the contemporary situation. This meal too has its very real eschatological significance for the disciples taking part:

> Truly I say to you, I shall not drink again of the fruit of the vine until that day when I drink it new in the kingdom of God. (Mk. xiv.25)

One thing is of even greater importance, however, and that is the significance of the blood and wine for the "many," i.e. for the peoples of the earth. The word spoken over the cup implies a covenant, a covenant sealed by "His blood," which is valid not only for the people of Israel as it once was but for all peoples; it implies also that the former covenant granted by

God is both superseded and fulfilled in the contemporary action; it implies finally that this extension of the covenant to the "many" is bound up with the circle of those to whom the word is spoken and who drink from the cup. The word spoken over the cup points beyond itself, therefore, in several directions. It indicates a turning away from the Jewish people who formerly were the partner in the divine covenant and celebrated it with the blood of sacrificial animals, and a turning towards the peoples who in His "new" covenant will be partners; and the sign of both is the action in the tiny circle of His own followers, who are thereby placed in an extraordinarily significant position. They are His friends in the present meal which is also an eschatological meal, they are citizens of the kingdom and guests in God's House, they are heirs of God's former covenant with His people and at the same time representative partners in God's covenant with the "many." All of these ideas are gathered up and comprehended in this action, this ceremony of eating and drinking together. Here clearly, in spite of the uniqueness of the occasion, is the makings of a cultic and eschatological ceremony. It originates in a divine covenant to which the Jewish cult also could appeal; it is based, as its Jewish equivalent was, on the God-given power of shed blood; and at the same time in its very "similarity" and in a formidable and eloquent silence it abrogates the whole sacred institution of sacrifice once and for all. In place of God's covenant with a people we have His covenant with the many; in place of the sacrificial blood of animals we have the blood of the Master; in place of a daily and yearly repetition we have a once-for-all death, a final and ultimate sacrifice. Here in the uniqueness and yet ordinariness of the occasion and in the eschatology of the meal the essence of the whole affair becomes manifest, the essence which renders completely invalid all the sanctity of the former cult and mediates an eschatological sanctity to those who are brethren in tribulation and expectation as a gift to them and a challenge. God's Kingdom, God's House, are established as it were in the context of human nourishment and ordinary pious usage; Temple and sacrifice in the isolated splendour and rich sanctity of their service come to an end.

Looking back over our study of the clear cultic references

and attitudes that we find in Jesus' Gospel, we find ourselves at all points asking the same question; what is it that cancels out the sanctity of an ancient, traditional cult and guarantees greater sanctity to the eschatological Gospel? We find also that Jesus Himself has answered the question briefly and mysteriously in the words: "something greater than the Temple is here," and that these words are interpreted by other sentences cast in a similar form and mean that *He* is greater than the Temple as He is greater than the prophet Jonah and King Solomon (Mt. xii.6,41f.). The trilogy priesthood, prophethood, kingship is therefore "fulfilled" in Him; and yet the categories "more" or "greater" are puzzling, for were not all three the gift of God and can one really make value judgments in these circumstances? Clearly this "more" does not belong to the plane of history; it is an analogical device to enable Jesus to express something eschatological and unspeakable. In virtue of the eschatological power inherent in His life and work He incorporates in Himself a trilogy, God's holiness, God's truth, God's glory.

There is one saying of Jesus which appears to bear direct witness to the holy foundation of His work and at the same time to point beyond it, and that is the saying: "the Son of man came not to be served but to serve, and to give his life as a ransom for many" (Mt. xx.28). The saying, very variously interpreted, and quite frequently rejected, is usually explained as meaning that Jesus' death was a sacrifice which He made on God's altar as the priest made sacrifice of the animal in the Temple, that He was therefore both priest and sacrifice, and sacrifice no longer for the one people but for the "many," for all peoples. The one word "ransom" is not nearly strong enough, however, to bear this meaning, and the echo of the Servant-song in Isaiah liii, is so clearly discernible that obviously "to give his life" means merely in a general sense "to die on behalf of others." Again the word "serve" has nothing to do with the old cult, it is obviously set over against a "lording" or even an actual "lordship" which might have been encountered in priests but more especially belongs to the kings and great men of the earth. Only if one can press the meaning "to serve at table" can one perhaps see an allusion to the meal celebrated by Jesus, which stands in profound eschatological opposition to the familiar holiness of the cult.

It is perhaps at first sight somewhat surprising to find so few cultic elements in the Gospel picture of Jesus, especially when we think of the rich embroidery of cultic motifs in the Epistle to the Hebrews and also in the Johannine literature. Probably the truth is that here too the saying about the stone which the builders rejected holds good; the very absence of cultic connexions emphasises all the more impressively the true measure of the opposition to cult and points to its eventual overthrow. The works that now fill the picture are not works of sanctification or of sacrifice but works of healing and proclamation, invitation and instruction, service and calling. They are done in a context not of exclusiveness but of everyday life. Jesus casts out demons as "your sons" cast them out. This explains the atmosphere of complete understanding and intelligibility which seems to pervade all His sayings and parables. At the same time it must be said that the works are done on a plane far more exalted than any to which the old cult ever aspired. It is the plane on which community and cult are revealed afresh according to God's eschatological "counsel." Jesus appoints the twelve disciples judges for the end-time, He invites sinners to God's table, eats with tax-collectors, and certainly where He is Himself host, entertaining His own followers or the people, there we see as in a glass darkly the new community and its new festival. There are of course many elements in Jesus' ministry which are directed against the traditional cult. Whereas it was fundamental to the latter that Jerusalem was the holy city and the dwelling place of God, the emphasis in Jesus' ministry is on Galilee: it is there that the "dawn from on high" has appeared. The miracles and the words of Jesus make Galilee the eschatologically consecrated land. We read of Capernaum's being "exalted to heaven" (A.V.). Whereas formerly priests were judges in Israel, now it is Galilean fishermen who are to fill the post. Clearly the opposition to the cult is connected already in Jesus' lifetime with the election of Galilee and the rejection of Jerusalem. But however far the opposition goes it is subsidiary to the great fact: "the kingdom of God has come near to you." By what is this fact guaranteed?

Jesus is a teacher and Master—rabbis call Him friend

and foe—journeying through the Jewish cities and villages
instructing as He goes.   If His teaching is disturbing and quite
different from the teaching of the Scribes it is because, in the
familiar words: "He taught as one who had authority."   And
this saying covers His whole eschatological Gospel and links
up at the same time with the Old Testament prophets, which
is the context, of course, in which the people see Him.   What
therefore He says about the cult often appears as a reflexion
of the Old Testament prophets' polemic against sacrifice and
the priesthood, and it is naturally not accidental that quotations
from the polemic appear in Jesus' teaching.   The parable of
the Wicked Husbandmen classifies the "son" as the last of the
series of God's messengers.   This is of course the reason for the
gospel of the Kingdom's becoming detached from the person
of the proclaimer and taking the form of a set of unforgettable
words and images, for purity of heart being set over against
purity by sacrifice and fasting, and the commandment of love
over against laws concerning burnt offerings and sacrifices.
But the Old Testament prophets never sought to overthrow the
priestly service in Jerusalem, nor did they ever overthrow it
in fact—Jeremiah or Ezekiel bear clear testimony to that.
They wanted something else alongside, or else in their passionate
loyalty to it they superimposed upon the cult: "He has showed
you, O man, what is good; and what does the Lord require of
you but to do justice, and to love kindness, and to walk humbly
with your God."   In Jesus' preaching, however, the opposition
to Temple and sacrifice is so fierce and fundamental that the
whole cultic order is set at nought and also stripped of the very
thing God gave it as its grace and its business: the priestly
work of the forgiveness of sins.   More than that, its end and
its destruction are clearly prophesied.   But it is not in a
prophet's power to say and do all this.   To remove the cult
is to set aside something which God instituted and to dissolve
a fellowship which God established.   Then it is not a teacher
who says and does these things, and equally not a prophet who
has appropriated a word of God.   It is not a people's Messiah
who does it, a Messiah freeing his people from misery and
unrighteousness and preparing them for that sacred eternity
in which they will dwell with God and He with them; for He
can and will only do his Messiah's work within the framework

of the nation and its historical experience of God, and by his work he will do no more than bring to fruition what God has been causing to grow through the centuries. The one who does this is one who has power to reject this nation and its foundation and upon a new foundation to build a new eschatological people of God. It is the Son of Man who alone can speak like this and act like this, for in terms of the visions of the Book of Daniel the Son of Man combines in His person this trilogy: king, judge, priest. Those three functions have found an impersonal kind of expression in the Temple, which is the house of kingly government, and of justice, and of sacred worship. Therefore it is competent for Him who calls Himself Son of Man to set Himself against this building for all its aura of sanctity and revelation: "I will destroy this Temple; upon this rock I will build my Church." Likewise it is the struggle against the cult and the overthrow of it which time and again pierces the mystery of the Son of Man and reveals Him as the power and guarantee of a new holiness. This same struggle produces a wonderful union, the union of the gospel of God's eschatological Kingdom and House with the fact of the eschatological Son of Man, so that the rabbi is able to work as the Son of Man would work, and the Son of Man is able to proclaim His message as a teacher or a rabbi would. And it all means just this: that the coming, the existence of the Kingdom of God is now. This contemporaneousness of the Kingdom gives holiness and hidden might to the ministry of the Son of Man, and finality and clear authority to the preaching of the teacher. Out of this dualism there grows—as the clearest proof of it and unmistakable witness to it—that which overthrows all cult and founds it "afresh": the celebration of the meal which is both an everyday meal and an eschatological celebration on the part of the elect people of God. In this institution, which makes a new thing of an ordinary pious usage and sanctifies it with the power of the eschatological Kingdom, we find the victory and authority that is characteristic of the eschatological "hour," which establishes the here and now as the beginning of the time of fulfilment in God's Kingdom and in God's House. One may perhaps hear an echo of that in the great saying: "The Son of Man came not to be served but to serve," i.e. strictly to serve at table. In that case the Lord's Supper

G

would really represent the ultimate meaning and the ultimate reality of the eschatological mission of the Son of Man.

The saying quoted above goes on in the familiar words, ". . . and to give his life as a ransom for many." The question arises therefore whether the death of Jesus also belongs to this great context of conflict with the cult. Certain links are fairly obvious. It is the champions of the cult who arrest Jesus, sit in judgment upon Him and "crucify Him"; one can gauge from these circumstances the measure of the enmity that had grown up between the chief priests as the lords and guardians of the Temple and Jesus their opponent. They also serve to bring into bold relief certain other questions concerning the history of Jesus' last days, but they indicate no more than a concrete historical set of events and tell us nothing about a basis for this death in the theology of the cult itself. Again if one looks for evidence of this in Jesus' own words we find they are singularly unhelpful, and references to the cult mostly concern actual cultic practices. Jesus' death is nowhere described as a sacrifice as Paul later describes it (Rom. III.25, etc.). Where Jesus announces His death He confines Himself to the words: "the Son of Man must be delivered into the hands of sinful men" (Lk. IX.44, XXIV.7). The expression "sinful men" does truly conjure up the picture of those who are enemies of the God whose "holiness" the priests and their sacrifices are meant to preserve, and there is no doubt a good deal of significance in the fact that the terms "sinful men," "men," and the quite specific "chief priests and scribes" are interchangeable; but this is all too general to be capable of reference to particular cultic emphases. The night scene in Gethsemane suggests no ground for Jesus' death other than the will of God. "Thy will be done"; the words we read speak only of the impenetrable mystery of the fact:

The hour is at hand, and the Son of man is betrayed into the hands of sinners.

Even the parable of the Wicked Husbandmen does not really reveal any cultic ideas, in spite of the fact that it is God's House and God's Kingdom that are its essential theme. The death of the only son really has more affinity with a theology of martyrdom than with anything else, with the idea that in all ages the wickedness of "the world," at war with the power and holiness of God, has persecuted and killed the messengers sent by God to the world. It may be of considerable significance that it is specifically against the Temple and the priesthood that this martyr-thinking is directed, but then our question about the connexion between this death and the cult is still being answered in very general terms. The only words which disclose any part of the mystery of this death are those spoken at the Last Supper: "My blood of the covenant, which is poured out for many." Again the language is too general to permit a straightforward analogy between Jesus' blood and the blood of the sacrificial animal, but the more exact description of His blood does lead us to that from which the cult also derives its holy authority and the sanctifying power of its worship. A covenant was once concluded on Sinai, it instituted for the Jewish people Temple and sacrifice, and it was sealed with blood. Those words spoken over the cup speak also of a covenant, which is as before ratified with blood, but it avails not for the people whom the Jewish cult sanctified by means of sacrificial blood but for the profane Gentiles which that cult excluded. It is, as a prior saying has it, "the many" who "will come from east and west and sit at table with Abraham, Isaac, and Jacob in the kingdom of heaven" (Mt. VIII.11). Perhaps there is still more to be gleaned from the words spoken over the cup. Certainly the words "poured out for many" is almost a literal repetition of the phrase used of the Servant of God in Isaiah LIII, who "poured out his soul to death" and "bore the sin of many." His death is a martyr's death, his life a ministry that God alone understands, and he bore life and death "for our transgressions." His hiddenness therefore is like the hiddenness of the Son of Man. If now the martyr's death of the servant serves for the blotting out of sins, and if the mystery surrounding the Son of Man is necessarily related to the struggle with and defeat of the cult, which is itself a service for the blotting out of sins, then ways open up of uniting the persons of the Servant and the Son of Man. The suffering and death of the Servant would become an essential part of the Son of Man concept, and both would be based not only on the idea of hiddenness but also on an essential opposition to that other "forgiveness of sins" which was in the grace and favour of the Jewish cult and was its task. It may be therefore that Matthew is interpreting correctly when he adds to the words spoken over the cup: "for the forgiveness of sins." Nevertheless the traces of this connexion are somewhat slight and uncertain. One last point emerges from the Last Supper and it is this: the death of Jesus represents obedience to a law ancient in Israel's history, or better it represents obedience to the ever-present will of God which was once norm and reality for the nation and for their cult, and now will be norm and reality for the eschatological community. Out of this dying there arises with the eschatological covenant made by God, the "new" cult, the celebration of the meal which is and also will be an eating and drinking "with me in my Father's kingdom" (Mt. xxvi.29).

In spite of these various links one may still perhaps feel that no vital connexion has been established between Jesus' death and the struggle against the cult, and it is true that one can point to nothing definite and unmistakable. Yet even the apparent vagueness and generality of these links is perhaps profoundly important. It is the performance of the will of God that is the ultimate and only aim of Jesus' works and proclamation, not merely the struggle against the cult, and the will of God is becoming word and event. In the struggle the overthrow of Temple and sacrifice is already fulfilled; in the overthrow there is to be seen also the "yes" to the grace of God which from the beginning and also through the cult was granted to the nation, and in virtue of which the members of the nation or perhaps only its fathers were changed into guests at God's table in God's House and Kingdom. As Jesus in His lifetime never called Himself a priest or performed the priestly function, so also He does not call Himself in death a sacrifice. His words: "your sins are forgiven" are spoken out of the infinite freedom and infinite obedience of the hidden Son of Man. His death likewise comes of a willing obedience to an eschatological purpose of God, unsearchable and necessary, as the Gethsemane story shows. The necessity of this death is part of that mystery which surrounds Him to the last and only then departs from Him. The early community rightfully and most meaningfully recounted that at His death "the curtain of the temple was torn in two, from top to bottom." It is a sign of the eschatological significance of this death, it is also only one sign among others, and teaches very plainly that in this struggle about which we have been speaking, the victorious struggle with the cult, we encounter "something greater than the temple." In the mystery that pertains to Him the Son of Man far transcends the Temple, and in life and death reaches towards a House of God and a Kingdom of God in an eschatological reality that makes them truly greater than all temples.

IV. CULT AND GOSPEL

WE have become acquainted with a wealth of material bearing upon the relationship between cult and Gospel, and we have isolated many aspects of it, both historical and objective. It will now be necessary to dispose all this within the whole framework of the story of Jesus and within the whole picture we have of Him. It will also be necessary to extend the framework, however, since we are speaking about the Gospel and the Gospel begins, according to the Evangelists, not with Jesus but with John the Baptist. His message and his work are "the beginning of the gospel" (Mk. 1.1). Again the witness of the Evangelists is also the witness of the early community living by faith in the Lord and by His words. Therefore we cannot ignore the attitude either of the "forerunner" or of those who came later in seeking to determine as fully and as accurately as possible the attitude of Jesus.

The difficulty of treating the problem of cult in the work of John the Baptist is not inconsiderable. Our records of him are scanty and vague. And yet perhaps these are sufficient for our purpose. The fact that John's parents were of the priestly class, that his work was carried out far from the nation's holy place in the sinister and unholy wastes of the wilderness, that his food and clothing, both of them important in priestly and cultic holiness, contravened all convention, that his preaching was an attack on the presumptuous complacency of his countrymen (born of the seed of Abraham) all of these things clearly suggest a question mark against the divine right of the Jewish cult, and seem to create an atmosphere of such scorn of cultic institution and cultic sanctity, that one is compelled to proceed to ask what is the relationship between John's baptism and the Jewish cult. There are many connecting links. The sacrifices offered in Jerusalem point continually and prophetically to the liturgy that will be sustained gloriously and eternally in the coming world; so too John's baptism is a sign of an eternal liturgy that will be done in the future by a holy community before God; and as in the one, blood made a mysterious provisional reference to what was coming, so in the other did water. Nevertheless as eschatological signs both sacrifice and baptism, however they may be superseded, are means granted "by heaven" preparing the way for the people to come to God and God to the people. In sacrifice—as we saw earlier—God acts, forgives His people their sins, and heals their diseases, so that they stand before Him as a holy, angelic company born anew. The essence of this atoning sacrifice cannot be better expressed than in the words used to define John's baptism: "repentance for the forgiveness of sins" (Mk. 1.4). In order that the divine action will be effective human co-operation is necessary in both cases. As it is men who make the sacrifice, so it is those who wish for baptism who submerge themselves in the running water. And yet of course the act of purification depends ultimately not on man but on God. Nevertheless God does not act without some measure of mediation. Certainly God's action depends on those making the sacrifice, whether it is the people or an individual; but equally certainly the salvation which God has bound up with sacrifice is made available to the sacrificers only through a mediator. The priest is the one commissioned for this mediation, particularly the High Priest, who on the Day of Atonement in the Holy of Holies sprinkles the blood of sacrifice for the sins of the nation. As he represents the nation before God, so he represents God before the nation. Indestructible holiness is vested in him, he bestows atonement and blessing, he is God's holy representative upon earth. In baptism God acts through a mediator, and the mediator is John who can say: "*I* baptise with water." This baptism also grants sanctification to the baptised person. The Baptist is also the representative of God in whose name he baptises and preaches. In Jewish terms he is therefore the high priest of baptism.

The relationship between the two is in fact so close, baptism is so clearly the eschatological counterpart of sacrifice, that a virtually impossible situation is created. Both claim to be of God, for the Jewish people and for the same purpose. Are they not mutually exclusive? Sacrifice is the medium of a holy cult and a holy community. There is therefore only this one true liturgy, and any other liturgy that claims to fill this role is idle falsehood like the worship of the heathen. With the same absolute validity baptism is the one true way to fellowship with God and all other ways lead astray, away from God. Sacrifice and baptism therefore become fierce rivals. Inasmuch as they have the same divine (not human) properties it seems they must do battle on Jewish soil for their very existence, their existence as things not human but divine. But surely one realises it is an unequal struggle when one considers that that which vindicates the divine efficacy of sacrifice, and the sanctification of the person sacrificing and of all the faithful, is ultimately the fact of a historical tradition and faith in a divine origin and a divine character. Baptism has none of these advantages; it has no tradition, it belongs to the now of the eschatological today which is breaking in. It is set over against all tradition as the coming world is set over against the present world. In face of this all sanctity associated with sacrifice evaporates therefore. Baptism is not limited to one particular holy place. It can take place anywhere where there is a stream of water or a spring, at home or abroad. It does not belong to the context of superb Temple buildings and glorious ceremonies; it requires for its performance only the baptist and the baptised and running water. It is not repeated, as sacrifice is, for all the vicissitudes of life or history; it is done once and it sanctifies the whole man provisionally until the impending fulfilment of baptism by the Spirit. All this speaks clearly for the eschatological character of John's baptism and the rejection of the historical character and divinity of the Jewish cult.

The career of John the Baptist with which "the Gospel" begins, really marks the first appearance of the problem of cult and Gospel; and the solution is important, for baptism and its eschatology involve the destruction of the whole complex fabric of the Jewish cult, woven of historical event and divine action, and therefore attached to time and place, nation and city. In the ruggedness of John's preaching and of his work, in the almost bizarre austerity of his appearance, his shunning of the things of man and his seeking after the things that are not of man, in all this we have the clear evidence of radical reaction. Nevertheless baptism with water is only provisional; it will be followed by baptism with the Spirit as surely as noon follows morning; but if it gives way to a world of abiding spiritual fulfilment then it passes away like any other historical act of God. It is the threshold of this coming world, a crossing, a passing over; but if it is to have the destructive and saving significance which the Baptist proclaims, would it then not be of necessity the final work of holy conversion? Again baptism takes place once, its grace is given and received in a moment; what power or norm does it offer for guidance through the continuing course of life? It involves merely a baptist and a baptised: what power or norm is there for binding them together in holy fellowship? The fact is, of course, that all these questions are resolved in the coming baptism with the Spirit which makes baptism with water all the more clearly a historical contrivance on the same dark level of life and history as the Jewish cult. It does not yet in fact produce any eschato-logically chosen community or any eschatological norm by which the community might be constituted and bound together, it is merely a solitary "cultic" act. And, however vigorously the burden and constraint of monstrous cultic ceremonial is cast off in baptism with water, really the cult concept is preserved to a certain extent and it is only the immediate expectation of the eschatological baptism by the Spirit that affects it. This indeed is the only guarantee of its claim to be "from heaven," and with sovereign contempt of human works and lowly reverence before God all historical guarantees are rejected. And yet the Baptist might have sought to be the warranter and fulfiller of his work even if the last shadow of human action was to be dispersed before the pure divine light of this baptism. The Baptist however merely humbled himself all the more before the "one coming after," "the thongs of whose sandals I am not worthy to stoop down and untie." In this humility before the now of the eschatological day we have the reason for this baptism's becoming so important for Jesus and for the early community.

As the Baptist's struggle was connected with the place of his appearance, the wilderness, so Jesus' struggle against the cult was in a remarkable and significant way connected with the borderland of Galilee. In my book *Galiläa und Jerusalem* I made the point that in the earliest days of Christianity Galilee came to be considered as the chosen place of eschatological fulfilment. It gained this distinction as Jesus' home and the scene of most of His ministry. Through these things this "borderland" is relieved of the stigma of uncleanness and obtains eschatological holiness. But such a view is also necessary in explaining the effectiveness of Jesus' work. When in the first story of healing in Mark's Gospel Jesus allows Himself to be called "the Holy One of God," when, as if in confirmation of the title, He forgives sins, sups with tax-collectors, and fails to observe fasts and Sabbaths, then the stand taken against the cultic institutions of Judaism is not by any means casual or haphazard—on the contrary. Because by virtue of His work a new holiness and a new salvation is coming, the traditional holiness with its multiplicity of rules falls to the ground. And Jesus has explicitly stated that His acts sanctify and exalt the places where they occur:

And thou, Capernaum, which art exalted to heaven.

(Mt. XI.23, A.V.)

What would appear at first to be merely a geographical contrast turns out to be something more. We have on the one hand at Jerusalem the traditional holiness of the cult, on the other hand in Galilee an eschatological holiness, and the source of it is the work and witness of the Master.

This same contrast helps to explain yet another problem which we encounter in the story of Jesus. It has often been asked—it was asked even in John's Gospel (VII.1-13)—why Jesus left Galilee, the place of eschatological fulfilment, and made His way to Jerusalem. Several reasons have been suggested. It has been said that Jerusalem is the holy centre of land and people, that Jesus' work would have been incomplete had He not pursued it and completed it there. Or else it has been held that Jesus went to Jerusalem as a dutiful Passover pilgrim. None of these reasons is completely satisfying. None of them explains, for example, Jesus' triumphal entry into the Temple and His cleansing of the Court of the Gentiles. Only the conflict with and the will to conquer the Jerusalem cult explains these things, conditioned perhaps by the thought, at once prophetic and apocalyptic, that the eschatological destiny of the nations and of Israel would be fulfilled at the holy Temple. That alone explains His taking possession of the sanctuary as Lord and keeper, and His cleansing of God's house that it might be the eschatological place of prayer "for all nations." And of course it is not by chance that it is the Temple area which is the scene of that series of questions and arguments that revolve so critically around the problems of cultic sanctification. In this conflict, moreover, the true objectives of the Jerusalem episode are revealed. The Jewish Temple authorities and the Jewish priesthood, to whom the eschatological destruction is announced display all the marks of aggressors; it is they who take Jesus prisoner, and it is they who hand Him over for crucifixion—even at the foot of the Cross priests are among the passers-by who cry mockingly: "You who would destroy the Temple and build it in three days, save yourself," and saving is again a cultic function. For His part Jesus sees this death coming and accepts it as the necessary condition of a "covenant for many." But this death also makes null and void the Jewish cult: the veil of the Temple is rent, the Holy of Holies is profaned.

One can object that some of this is a reflexion of the mind of the early Christian community rather than of the mind of Jesus Himself, and that may be to a certain extent true; but what may represent the mind of the community is also clearly in this connexion the reasserting of an antithesis already of long standing, an antithesis which in embryo determined both Jesus' message and His ministry. We must now examine this antithesis more closely.

Cult and Gospel—it is not only history that links them together, it is also their content. The Jewish cult necessitated, as we have seen, the idea and the fact of eschatological fulfilment. In it a revelatory and sanctifying act of God in the past had become wedded to the continuing power of an historical event and produced that mysterious wonder, a holy service which granted to the nation salvation and holiness. The cult was therefore regarded as superior to all historical and natural forces that limit the life of a nation. It not only freed Israel from sin and uncleanness but claimed to banish sickness and want and oppression and death (all the things that contradicted holiness) from the land and people within which it operated. Holiness meant, in a historical sense and in faith, life pure and undisturbed: sin therefore meant for individual and nation, for city and country, hunger and need and suffering and death. The Temple at Jerusalem had to be the place which not only resolved the tangle of oppression and suffering mysteriously and yet immovably, but also overcame them with the cleansing power of the holy God. And had it in fact been such a place, the foundation upon which it rested would have collapsed; for of course as itself an historical phenomenon it was subject to all the natural and historical conditions of human existence, and as representing God's sanctifying and cleansing act it was lord and conqueror of these things. In the nature of the case, therefore, there was here a longing for that eschatological fulfilment which would tear down the veil that divided historical event and divine action, and would change the exclusiveness and speciality of sacred ceremonial, preserved as such in history, into the pure and universally applicable reality of an eternal liturgy.

The eschatological Gospel also presupposes the sacred fact and historical speciality of a cult, however, for it would not be the final fulfilment but at best a beautiful dream were it not to comprehend in itself and unite all the forces which in all the confusion of historical existence nevertheless represented the holy sparks of the divine flame. It is the end brought about by God only because the beginning (these forces and institutions) was given by God. Among the various forms once ordained by God, however, among the sanctities claimed for city and land, individual and nation, commandments and promises, things done and things seen, the sanctity of the cult is if not the greatest then certainly among the greatest. One can never remain silent about the cult in the Gospel, therefore, one must ask questions and seek in the word of the Gospel the appropriate answer. What the Gospel answer is to the complex question posed by the cult is the crucial problem.

One can gather how closely integrated cult and Gospel are from this fact alone, that the proclamation of the nearness of the Kingdom of God is a proclamation of the coming House of God or City of God which those who hear will enter; and if this is the essential content of Jesus' message taken as a whole then clearly cultic ideas are at the heart of it. The essence of the message is that the eschatological Kingdom and House possess the sanctifying power which was inherent incompletely and insufficiently in the Jewish cult. Those things can be fulfilled which the national sanctuary had only promised, and things can be loosed which in spite of daily sacrifice remained bound. If, however, this eschatological House of God fulfils all that has gone before, then clearly it is also sharply and inexorably inimical to it as the complete is always inimical to the incomplete. The Temple at Jerusalem was regarded as God's house among His people; this eschatological *basileia* is the holy place of all who will be God's guests and children. The prototype fellowship that was found in the Old Testament is completely taken over into the "new" House of God. This Kingdom means for it truly a *consummare* and *elevare*, a "destroying and building again." This fellowship is therefore the true eschatological community of God within the historical people of God. And yet it reaches also far beyond this nation because God is the God not only of this one nation but of all nations, and this fulfilment is the fulfilment of the entire work of Creation—which was indeed the claim for the Temple at Jerusalem. It was the one and only place of true worship where God sanctified men, and therefore it was the sacred centre of nations and men. This eschatological fellowship comprehends the lost sheep of the house of Israel and the lost of the Gentile world: "Many will come from east and west and sit at table with Abraham, Isaac, and Jacob in the kingdom of heaven" (Mt. VIII.11). So there can come into being the wedding-party community of God which includes both the nation and the nations, and elects men from both to be guests and children in God's house.

One will object that the Gospel is a message, and that however urgently and powerfully it may be proclaimed word alone cannot cause something to disintegrate which has been sanctified for centuries and made the nation's foundation. Undoubtedly the objection is to a certain extent justified, as we shall see, and yet at the moment it is more important that the message concerning God's House and Kingdom does in fact usurp the place and authority of the Jewish Temple, as Jesus' words to the man sick of the palsy show: "Your sins are forgiven." All this has its counterpart in an impressive Old Testament insight. God is in control, as He often reveals, and no human reasoning can determine the form of word or of action by which He may make Himself known: "I will be what I will be" (Ex. III.14, note). Where He "is," however, His revelation is valid unconditionally. The Old Testament prophets always proclaimed this. Therefore the revelatory word of the Gospel can dislodge even the firmly established, sacred power of Temple and sacrifice. One may compare also the concrete, the so to speak historical-eschatological situation in which Jesus finds Himself, coming after the Baptist. John had set eschatological baptism over against sacrifice; only baptism with the Spirit and fire could follow his work and this would bring fulfilment not only for baptism with water but also for the world and for men. Jesus stands between the time of baptism with water and that of baptism with the Spirit; His work, for all its eschatological power, is human and historical. In so far as His work includes the preaching of the Gospel—to preach the Gospel "is why I came out" (Mk. 1.38)—He hits on the only possible medium, the medium of the word of the Kingdom of God spoken in the space between the still existing fact of earth and the approaching fact of consummation. In other words, the Gospel unites the revelation proclaimed in the Law and the prophets with the eschatological revelation of God's House. It can therefore find good in that first revelation, in its commandments and promise, and must at the same time review critically all cultic rites and duties that belong to it. Jesus can speak as a prophet before the holy God and as a teacher submitting to the holiness of God's revealed will: in God's word in the Torah and in prophecy God's holy revelation is more genuine than in human action. The Gospel is often, therefore, merely "eschatologised" challenge and promise, but the word in it concerning the Kingdom of God that is at hand changes even the Law, since it is no longer guarded and supported by means of a holy sacrifice. When the mighty cry rings out: "Repent, for the kingdom of God is at hand"— which is indeed analogous to the cultic custom of penitence before every festival—it is obvious that the Gospel does purify and refine the Law with eschatological thoroughness, and removes from it all that smacks of human or historical conditions. Divorce is not countenanced: it was only allowed "because of the hardness of your hearts." The variety and multiplicity of commandments fade away or are comprehended in the simple commandment concerning love. This simplicity is at the same time the eschatological seal of God's House and

Kingdom. Likewise and for the same reason the Gospel demands of men what is virtually impossible:

You must be perfect, as your heavenly Father is perfect.

and demands it (because of the eschatological power in the message) as the one thing possible and necessary. It trains its beam on the whole man, on the "heart," which determines man's words and deeds, his thinking and his inclination, which on the human level is imperfect and impenetrable and which by the grace of God alone can be mastered and can achieve any kind of wholeness and wholesomeness. So there takes place, as if it was the most natural thing on earth, that miracle which blends holiest law and man's heart of hearts in purity: love God and love your neighbour, a formula which is at once duty and gift, commandment and promise. It is born of the knowledge that now is the last day and the last hour; this "last" lifts everything into the light of that end which is also the beginning of the Kingdom of God. In the Gospel message everything historical is wedded to eschatological revelation, and becomes a unity in the same way as time and God's time are one in the actual act of proclaiming. The more the Gospel message approximates to teaching and prophecy, the more it becomes clear that the foundation is in that eschatological event; and the more it speaks in terms of the revelation of the Kingdom of God, the more urgent is its reaction against tradition.

It will be clear now that all power and holiness pales before the "last" of this Gospel. If one is able to speak of a holiness in which God's own House appears as it is meant to appear at the last, then all historical holiness is immediately dissipated like mist at the dawn. Where man stands before God in an existence that is stripped of all contingency, where his true humanity consists in his "pure" heart that is not subject to the limitations of time and the world, life and death, there a "new" holiness arises; and this holiness is that condition of immediate encounter with eschatological fulfilment which requires no mediation, not even the media of life and history.

Once again one may feel the force of the question, what guarantee has this Gospel message over against the massive power of the instituted cult? One thinks first of the demand for absolute and unconditional faith, and truly faith is an essential part of this message, faith in the nearness of the Kingdom of God. And faith is so powerful that Jesus can attribute to it what is really attributable only to the power of God:

> Have faith in God. Truly, I say to you, whoever says to this mountain, "Be taken up and cast into the sea" . . . it will be done for him.
>
> (Mk. xi.23)

Faith here is therefore not the guarantee of the Gospel, but the Gospel is the guarantee of faith. Besides even the cult requires faith, faith in its divine origin and its sacred power among the men who are its adherents. And this faith is guaranteed and well founded; it rests on a history which in spite of all catastrophes and confusions is God's history; it is the faith of a people who despite all uncertainty and uncleanness is nevertheless God's people. Did the word of the Master really have greater power than all this, was it in fact the ultimate reality that could destroy this most holy foundation—a word that was proclaimed in the name of the same God and Father who laid the said foundation? It becomes clear how difficult this matter of guarantee is. The eschatological Gospel disclaims it, but the historical cult which is set aside by its message clamours for it. Time and again in our Gospels we hear the question raised not only by enemies but even by the Baptist. And Jesus has answered it. He points to the power of His works which cleanse the land and the people of disease and demonic impurity:

> If it is by the finger of God that I cast out demons, then the kingdom of God has come upon you.

And yet effective as these works were, according to the Gospels, they do not answer our problem. They can lead to unbelief as well as to faith, to Beelzebub as well as to God; and we are left with that human and historical indeterminateness in which divine and demonic powers vie with one another in crazy disorder. Nor are the works eschatologically decisive—"your sons" also do them. When the paralytic was healed the crowds "glorified God, who had given such authority to men" (Mt. ix.8). The one sign which could infallibly authenticate the breaking in of eschatological fulfilment is the very one Jesus refuses to give: "Truly, I say to you, no sign shall be given to this generation" (Mk. VIII.12). Such renunciation involves Jesus' other works in a certain ambiguity, an ambiguity which remains until "the kingdom of God has come near," and in view of which the cult can appear as the true place of security against the assaults of demons and of "purification" from diseases. In truth the cult is involved in a similar ambiguity, but if the cult is to be overthrown then its functions, which hitherto were necessarily imperfect, must be preserved in a more perfect form. The struggle against Temple and cult therefore demands something which cannot be demanded: something really eschatological, gleaming with the light of a greater power and holiness than the cult had possessed or could possess.

Against this background the true profundity of the significance of those things which we found here and there in Jesus' proclamation and in His actual ministry will be appreciated. They do in fact represent the eschatological counterpart to the historical and divine cult. For example there is gathered around the Master the hidden eschatological community. It is a community of poor and oppressed, of sick and demon-possessed, of sinners and tax-collectors—all the people who, being excluded from the holy ordinances of the cult, were all the more intensely involved in the perils and perplexities of life. Those whom the cult excluded Jesus took to Himself, and those whom it banned from its solemnities Jesus blessed. Where the Temple erected barriers to preserve a traditional holiness Jesus flung them down to make available an eschatological holiness:

Come to me, all who labour and are heavy laden, and I will give you rest. (Mt. XI.28)

Another similar sign is to be found at the Temple itself. When Jesus cleansed it of money-changers and merchants, according to Mark He "taught" the people, or according to Matthew "the blind and the lame came to him in the temple, and he healed them." Formerly a place of ceaseless sacrifice, it is now consecrated as a place of prayer, and all its cultic ceremonies become meaningless in comparison with this one great office, the dialogue between man and God. And in place of the purity from sin which the Temple sought to bestow there is now the final and conclusive validity of Jesus' mighty

H

words: "Your sins are forgiven." The most profound of all elements, however, is the eschatological overthrow of the old and the foundation of a "new" cult in the institution of the Meal. It contains two ideas, the idea of natural nourishment of the body and the eschatological idea of the blessed feast at God's table, and both ideas are united in the contemporary fellowship. In one sense, therefore, the Meal is far removed from holiness as the Jewish cult honoured it. It is characterised by the usual and the familiar, even in its prayers and actions, and it can take place wherever men satisfy their hunger with thanksgiving to God and in fellowship with the Master. The homeliness of one's own house or the beauty of the countryside take the place of the holiness of a particular building with holy altar and sacred sacrifice. Inherent in this commonplace, however, there is also that community spirit which in God's Kingdom and household unites His elect in table fellowship. One does not yet ask how such unity is possible; the important thing is—if one may put it this way—the fact of the daring of reading into earthly hunger and a godly family's ordinary meal the unspeakable riches of an eternal feast with God. It happens only because it is the last hour and the time of the breaking in of fulfilment; it makes the ordinary the threshold of eschatological glory in which the Kingdom "has come near"; and it can turn to-day into God's eternal day because in the fellowship of the poor and the hungry, who gather round the Master, is prefigured the eschatological community of God's guests and children. It also introduces yet another element into the Meal, that of helpful brotherly love, which feeds the hungry and gives the thirsty to drink. Characteristically, too, the community idea has changed. The community is no longer thought of, as it was in the cult, in terms of a holy people, but in terms of the household and the family which is the kernel of God's community because it is the basic unit in life. The historical fellowship that the nation knew, even though it was founded by God, is broken up; the idea of fellowship is narrowed to match that of a household, and at the same time broadened to match that of a vast gathering in which God is Father and host and His own are children and guests.

In view of the at once unspeakably indeterminate and unspeakably determinate, i.e. eschatological character of the

Lord's Supper, one may ask whether its institution can really be regarded as an act which founds a new cult. The question has all the more justification in that a new cult would also necessarily mean the founding of a new community. And where do we find any express act of founding such a community? Indeed were one to find some hidden reference to it Jesus' clear forward-looking word would contradict it—forward-looking to an eschatological future that is at hand: "I will build another temple in three days; upon this rock I will build my Church." The question of the foundation of a new cult cannot be answered in a simple yes *or* no but only in a profound, eschatologically determined yes *and* no. Jesus was not establishing a cult in His Last Supper, i.e. a fixed and hallowed ordinance for the salvation of men. He was performing an act in which He was handing over to His disciples the thing that characterises His whole life and death:

As my Father appointed a kingdom for me, so do I appoint for you.
(Lk. XXII.29)

This Kingdom and Household is there hidden in the meal fellowship—this family meal perhaps helps us to see more clearly now why God's Kingdom is depicted as a house—just as previously it had been hidden in Jesus, until it will be "revealed" at the day of consummation. And this fellowship of disciples sharing the meal in brotherliness, no matter where it is, this is God's hidden community, hidden until it is "revealed" at the day of consummation. That complicated network of the divine and the historical which constituted the Jewish cult is unmistakably gone. Here are no priests, no Temple, no sacrifice, no fasts and pious practices, but the ever possible and ever necessary triad—a meal, prayer, and love. The unity which made the Jewish people the community of God and the community of God an historical people is likewise gone. In place of this traditional ordinance and this community there has come something which is held together by one power alone, the Gospel and Him who proclaims the gospel of the Kingdom of God. This power, in its demand and in its promises, in its claim and in its exhortation, is such that it cuts through all other human ties to make "new" and closer ones in this Meal. From this point of view one may say that the institution of the Lord's Supper does represent the foundation of a "new" cult, which itself creates a "new" fellowship; certainly we begin to see the old cult in an entirely new light. We see that it needs the Gospel, in view of its own inner tension, to be the power that makes cult; the Gospel, which does not only make demands as the Law does but also sanctifies as sacrifice does. It needs the word of God, that both commands and promises, which is the beginning of all created things, and also the end of all created things because it alone has the power to surmount time and space and to be superior to them. Finally it needs not only the gospel of the Kingdom of God, it needs also the preacher who can fill both the role of the prophet and the role of the bringer of eschatological fulfilment, who can say both: "The kingdom of God is near" and: "my Father has appointed the kingdom for me." The cult is an ordinance of the God whose Kingdom and House is now coming, and a divine actuality which nevertheless fades and disappears before the "Holy One of God."

Everything ultimately depends, therefore, on the one question, who this is who preaches and acts and works eschatologically. It is a question which the reader who is a man of faith may ask in many contexts. The important thing is that where cult and Gospel are concerned it is a necessary question, a question asked for a very definite reason and requiring a definite answer. Judaism personified its hopes for a time of fulfilment in several ways, dictated either by familiar patterns in its own history or by visions of unspeakable glory in the last days. We know the Messiah-king who will erect again the throne of David in a free and peaceful land. The 17th Psalm of Solomon has portrayed him in colours at once gleaming and intimate. But the majesty of this king, however triumphant and righteous, does not empower him to destroy an ordinance once sanctified by God. He can at most make such a thing free from blemish and impurity and thereby establish it afresh. This king merely executes that same will of God, the revelation of which in the history of the nation had remained as it were empty and will only at the end attain its true proportions. Here, however, we are not speaking of establishing but of destroying; the words are cutting like a knife's edge:

I will destroy this Temple.

We know also the Messiah-prophet. He does not have the

religio-political splendour of a king, he has the more intimate power of making the Jewish people a holy people by instruction and example. He can be a critic of the cult as many of the old prophets were, he can also make demands which do not belong to the sphere of Temple and sacrifice; but how could a Messianic prophet whose task is not to govern but to teach, not to fulfil but to prepare, how could he seek to undermine what God does in sacrifice? It is true that many aspects of Jesus' ministry remind us of this prophet figure—He also teaches, He knows the "way to eternal life"; but a Messiah-prophet could not say: "On this rock I will build my Church." Building is God's business not a prophet's. A prophet does not have a new church, he only knows the old church founded and sanctified by God, to which he himself belongs. Here again even any fundamental opposition to the cult is out of the question, let alone destruction and overthrow. Finally we know the Messiah-priest, who at the end banishes all uncleanness and spreads holiness abroad throughout the people. The nature of the expectation completely excludes the possibility that this person would undertake the unholy work of destroying the holy Temple; indeed his eschatological task binds him precisely to the existing cultic ordinances and arrangements. In all of the above one thing is presupposed: their work, however messianically glorious, bases itself on the divine acts which first created the people, the cult, the Temple, the priesthood, and the Law, and have preserved them through a long and exclusive history. This tradition is, so to speak, the air they breathe, without which they could not live, and certainly without which they could not bring to completion their work once begun by God. To seek to reject and overthrow the cult one must obviously be in an entirely different position and be concerned with an entirely different kind of holiness. The position occupied by this one who fulfils and at the same time destroys lies outwith all history; it is the place from which the last and final judgment comes in condemnation and blessing, in rejection and perfecting. Only in terms of the pure holiness of such a judge can the eschatological image of God's people and Kingdom and House be formed anew out of this tradition or in contrast to it—God's Kingdom and House in which the people will dwell with God and He with them.

Everything that happens to the cult, whether to its advantage
or to its detriment, clearly points to one requirement, someone
having God's power and holiness who will himself bring the
eschatological fulfilment. There is only one person known in
the Jewish faith, who by nature and not merely in virtue of a
special commission would be adequate for such work. He
comes from without this people and yet is sent to it, he is
powerful enough to change the ordinances of the cult or of the
Law and holy enough to sanctify a historical people. He is
the Son of Man. He is, as God is, king, judge, and high
priest—his flowing garment indicates this: "and with a golden
girdle round his breast" (Rev. 1.13); his power is his holiness
and his word is and brings eschatological fulfilment. Jesus
bore this very name. Because of it He is "the Holy One of
God." Admittedly at first sight there are difficulties. For
example when did we see Jesus ever doing what the Son of Man
of Dan. vii does, and where are we told that this Son of Man,
who destroys the kingdoms of the world and redeems the Jewish
people and makes them the community of the holy ones, will
destroy the cult? And yet to ask this question is to forget one
thing: that the Son of Man of Dan. vii is the revealed Son of
Man, who comes on the clouds of heaven, while here we are
dealing with the Son of Man who until the day of consummation must preserve His secret. The former perfects the
community and the world in revealed glory, the latter says
only: "I will build another temple." In other words Jesus'
historical work and His being in history constitute a distinction as well as a link between the idea of the hidden Son of
Man and that of Daniel's vision. In so far as both were bound
together in the idea of the eschatological secret there arises
that necessary and paradoxical unity which conceals the judge
of the end under the guise of a rabbi, and the destroyer of the
old cult and bringer of the "new" cult under that of a prophet
and physician. This view, which finds in the "Son of Man"
the holiness of God and His Kingdom and sees Him as a teacher
among the poor of His people, alone can solve the problem of
cult and Gospel; indeed it compels us to solve it.

This Son of Man idea is so inexhaustibly profound princi-
pally because of the dual nature of the Son of Man's secret.
From the point of view of the purely eschatological concept of

the Son of Man His historicity is the secret; from the point of
view of His historical actuality His true character as Son of Man
is the secret. This two-sided unity explains first of all why the
attack on the cult launched by the Baptist and his baptism was
inconclusive; both radically rejected Temple and sacrifice and
priesthood; but they could only point to the Coming One who
would baptise with the Spirit and to this baptism with the
Spirit, however radical they sought to be. Their "no" required
a firmer eschatological basis than baptism with water could
afford. Baptism with water indeed gave to the attack a more
clearly historical character than it dared have. The same is
true to a lesser extent of sacrifice in the Jerusalem Temple.
The abolition of both Temple and sacrifice requires more
than humility before what comes after. It requires a power
which will bring final salvation as a straightforward human
work. It requires one who in the hidden holiness of the
Kingdom of God preaches the gospel of this Kingdom and
lives it. Both things are expressed in Jesus' relationship to the
cult with exemplary clarity. On the one hand He exalts the
message of the eschatological Gospel to that higher plane of
holiness and purity where it passes judgment on the ordinances
of cultic holiness and overthrows them, and He surrenders
Himself to the eschatological power of this word of God in such
a way that it is detached from His person and He speaks as if
He were an Old Testament prophet or a Jewish rabbi. It is
only in the sovereign fashion in which binding cultic norms
and practices are neglected or changed that the truth about the
eschatological character and origin of this Gospel becomes
apparent. On the other hand with the authority of the Son of
Man He shares with tax-collectors and sinners, the poor and
the hungry, the people and the disciples, the feast which under
the guise of an everyday meal at once conceals and reveals the
eschatological marriage feast of the Lamb. And finally, as if
from the middle of these two sets of opposing factors, He can
announce what is in God's eschatological counsel and in His
eschatological power: "I will destroy this temple; upon this
rock I will build my Church." He can also in eschatological
fulfilment of the word of God in the Old Testament enter the
Temple at Jerusalem and cleanse its forecourt to make it a
house of prayer for all peoples. The apparent contradiction

involved in cleansing the very Temple that it is His eschatological commission to overthrow and to build "anew" merely
reflects the same mystery which pervades the concept of the
Son of Man, this *coincidentia oppositorum*, and is resolved therein.

The question of the cult is therefore helpful and more than
helpful for the understanding of the life and work of the Master.
Is it necessarily helpful for the understanding of His death?
Ideas readily occur which Paul developed and which the writer
of the Epistle to the Hebrews made, admittedly on different
premises, the kernel of his theology—ideas concerning Jesus'
voluntary and final sacrifice which puts an end to all Old
Testament sacrifice. We have seen, however, that there is no
word of Jesus' to justify such an idea. Indeed it would be an
inadequate idea since it would suggest that these same cultic
institutions were still binding which it was His whole life's
work to judge and to overthrow. Wherever we are told of the
necessity of Jesus' death a twofold reason is given: we are told
it was necessary because it was in God's eschatological purpose,
and because of the sin of men and nations. One can easily
see how these correspond in a remarkable way to the dual
mystery of the Son of Man. In the hearing before the Sanhedrin the connexion is made abundantly clear. The powerless
prisoner confesses:

> I am; and you will see the Son of man sitting at the right hand of Power,
> and coming with the clouds of heaven.   (Mk. xiv.62)

This confession convicts Him. In Jesus' passing from life to
death the process of eschatological fulfilment, as God has determined it, is both concealed and revealed. If the Master's life
and work marked the beginning of this process, then His death
is the mid-point or at least a continuation of God's eschatological action, preserving as much as revealing the former
mystery in the continuation. What hitherto in His life was
considered eschatological power and holiness is now to be
found in a greater and more significant degree in His death.
If His work and His preaching were destined to combat and
vanquish priesthood and Temple, then His death is the
continuation of this struggle and this victory. The significance
of the struggle is expressed, as we have seen, in the words:

> I will destroy this temple and in three days I will build another.

With Jesus' death the first half of this saying has become eschatological reality. With profoundly meaningful, eschatological consistency the Gospel record of the moment of Jesus' expiring reads: "And behold the curtain of the temple was torn in two, from top to bottom." It is a part of the mystery of the Son of Man that His death cannot be thought of as an interruption of His life and work but rather as a more intensive pursuit of that which was His life-work. The Son of Man goes as He came; His death continues the progress which His "coming" began. If it was His life's task to abolish the Jewish cult, then we must say that His death crowned this part of His work. It gives that finality to the victorious struggle against the cult which enabled Christianity to extinguish the sacrificial flame and destroy the temple wherever the Gospel took root.

Our discussion has thus led us almost imperceptibly into a consideration of the early Church, and here again from a different angle the importance of our topic becomes clear. One speaks so much of the breach between the history of Jesus and that of the early Church, which the death of Jesus constitutes, but the problem before us instructs us in a more accurate line of thinking—that indeed there is a strong connexion between Jesus' struggle against the cult and the attitude of the first Christians. That struggle has led us repeatedly from the Gospel to the person of the One proclaiming it and making it effective, and in the death of Jesus which brings to a tremendous end the work of the hidden Son of Man this Gospel has become, in the person of its champion, the beginning of actual eschatological fulfilment. In order to comprehend this more fully therefore we shall consider again briefly the earliest period of the primitive Palestinian community.

The material in the Book of Acts to which we must refer is admittedly somewhat scanty, and yet helpful enough in this respect that obviously Luke bases his account on eschatological presuppositions other than those of a theology of the Son of Man. The picture of the Christian community he presents is that of a Messianic sect, still a fairly integral part of Judaism, only practising within it a Jewish piety with a particular slant— faith in the *Parousia* of the crucified Lord and Master. We learn too that they assembled daily in the Temple and "did not cease teaching and preaching Jesus as the Christ" (Acts v.42). The original Christian community appears therefore to have forgotten the old antagonism to Temple and cult which both John the Baptist and Jesus had pursued, and to be relegating the questions concerning God's house and God's people to the eschatological future.

When one looks more closely, however, the first impression proves to be a mistaken one. Here again in Acts we find no reference to the first Christians participating in the daily sacrifice. It is true they assemble at hours of sacrifice, but when Peter heals a lame man at the ninth hour (which is also a sacrifice hour) and preaches the message concerning the Lord Jesus, he omits completely all reference to the sacrifice that is going on in the Court of the Priests and speaks to the people about the "Holy and Righteous One," whom "you denied," and exhorts them to repent and be converted, "that your sins may be blotted out." But it was for just such a purpose that the holy act of sacrifice was daily performed. Stephen recalls Jesus' words (and his face was like the face of an angel): "Jesus of Nazareth will destroy this place" which shows that the saying was current within the community; and the persecution which carried him to his martyr's death was extended to the whole community. The opposition to Temple and cult is still as sharp as ever it was in Jesus' lifetime. One finds a similar attitude even in much later times, an attitude characteristically different from Paul's, adopted by those who considered themselves the staunchest guardians of the heritage from Jesus and who nevertheless adhered strictly to the Jewish Law. Burkitt has dealt with this in his lectures, *Christian Beginnings*.[1] He concludes from the ancient account by Hegesippus of the martyrdom of James, the Lord's brother, that James did not take part in the Jewish sacrifice although (perhaps better because) he spent his days in the Temple praying for forgiveness of the sins of the people. We know that the later Nazarenes rejected all sacrifices, and in the so-called Gospel of the Ebionites we read the apocryphal saying attributed to the Lord and already quoted: "I am come to destroy sacrifice."

It seems a reasonable conclusion from these various references

[1] Leiden, 1924.

that the earliest Christian community—or at least sections of it—did reject Jewish cultic ordinances as their Master had done, and that they did so while still acknowledging the Torah, which was after all for Jesus also the way to life. Several other accounts confirm this attitude—all the more impressively really if in fact some of them are legendary. Hegesippus tells us for example that James, the Lord's brother, wore the linen garment proper to the High-Priestly office and did not hesitate to move about in the holy places reserved for priests alone. But if a layman from Galilee (still a proscribed territory) clothes himself and behaves like a priest of holy lineage then clearly it implies at least the claim to equal the Jewish priests in holiness and purity if not to excel them. From Epiphanias, who claims Clement of Alexandria and Eusebius as his sources, we learn that the same James wore the golden breast-plate of the High Priest, and Polycarp of Smyrna has the same story about the beloved disciple. From such accounts, whether they are true or legendary, one can only conclude that the early Christians continued to hold the view that with Jesus' death and resurrection the Jewish cult and the Jewish priesthood had been brought to an end; whatever God-given virtue had been in them had been transferred to the context of faith in the Master and His works and to certain leaders of the early Christian community as the true Israel.

The antagonisms that marked Jesus' history were preserved then in early Christianity. That alone can explain why we never find in the Gospel tradition any comment on the fact that the same Law which was honoured and obeyed as the will of God contained the cultic ordinances which were rejected. The one was so decisively isolated from the other by Jesus' words and by the facts of His history that before this holy actuality even the holiest cultic demands fell to the ground. The most profound explanation of the attitude of early Christianity is contained in the tradition concerning Jesus' death: "And the curtain of the temple was torn in two, from top to bottom" (Mk. xv.38), or as the Gospel of the Hebrews has it: "The lintel carrying the corner-stone of the sanctuary broke." The general sense of this is confirmed by similar Jewish references; it means the impending or actual destruction of the Temple. If, however, Jesus' death and the rending of the veil

here coincide then there is in the coincidence a special significance. Jesus was put to death on account of His utterances:
"I will destroy this temple." His death—so this miracle in the
Temple would seem to suggest—fulfilled this saying or began
to fulfil it in the same sense that it laid open for everyone to
see that which by God's will had been kept in holy darkness.
Because of this one can be confident that the second half of
Jesus' prophecy will also be fulfilled: "And in three days I will
build another." The early Christians' attitude reflects all this
exactly. They reject the cult, though daily in the Temple they
do not cease "teaching and preaching Jesus as the Christ."
These other obligations, which according to Jesus reveal the will
of God, are still observed: if anything they are more strictly
binding—every jot and tittle—now that the cult is nullified.
Stephen appears to have been the first to suggest that Christians
were exempt from these obligations too; he was accused of
saying something which does not occur in Jesus' original
saying: "And will change the customs which Moses delivered
to us" (Acts VI.14).

One recognises the importance of such an attitude for the
Gospel tradition when one realises that it formed the basis and
standard to a certain extent for the draft of the history of Jesus,
and therefore for the construction of the Gospels of Matthew
and Mark. It emphasises two things in particular: Galilee as
the place of holiness in contrast to the former holiness of the
city of Jerusalem, and the story of Jesus' suffering and death
as the story of Jesus' completing in His death, with revelatory
might, the work of overthrowing the Jewish cult begun in His
lifetime. Is it perhaps a sign of this that the story proceeds by
days and hours like the services and sacrifices on high and holy
cultic festivals, that its introduction is Jesus' entry into the
Temple and the story of the new consecration of the sanctuary,
which indeed the Fourth Gospel places at the beginning of
Jesus' ministry? It is this early Christian rejection of the cult
which explains the basic ideas and the topographical structure
of the Gospel material in Mark and Matthew. Jesus' life
becomes a progress to death, and with profound significance
the announcements of His suffering are placed at the very
point at which it is confirmed that Galilee and the adjoining
heathen territories are the eschatological holy places. It is also

the point at which the Meal is instituted in a twofold miracle, and Galileans and heathen are united as the "new" hidden community of the holy ones.   The form and content of the first two Gospels—in characteristic contrast to Luke's Gospel—are illumined therefore by the problem of cult and Gospel within them.   It would be easy and rewarding to account for the origin and arrangement of the Gospel material in detail; for the moment, however, the early community's basic attitude is more important.

One understands it even better when one examines the fundamentals which governed its life.   These are not merely faith in the crucified and risen Lord and expectation of His *Parousia*, but also two eschatological cultic ceremonies, once-and-for-all baptism and the daily Meal.   Both are practised from the beginning; both stand in opposition to the cult and overthrow it.   The Meal in particular, which is at once the Lord's Meal, a brotherly service, and a love-feast, becomes the immovable basis of all faith and hope and contains within itself and within every celebration a firm rejection of sacrifice and priesthood.   They know, these Christians, that in this, the Lord's feast, they are united and sanctified as His holy eschatological community when they celebrate it "with glad and generous hearts" (Acts II.46).   One finds here too the explanation of the name which the early Christians bore, and for which many analogies can be found in legal and apocalyptic as well as Old Testament sources, but no satisfactory reasons.   Formerly the cult elevated the Jewish people to the status of a holy people; so now in conscious opposition to sacrifice and on the basis of faith in the eschatological Meal those who share it are "the holy ones" as the Master was and is "the Holy One of God."   The name is consciously and essentially bound up with the problem of cult and Gospel.

Besides being called the "holy ones" the early Christians were also called the "poor."   The reason for this name is, as we have seen, the same.   The name does however disclose another historical perspective to which some further reference might have been made.   It indicates that circle of those first Christians who represent Galilee and Galilean piety.   For them Galilee is the holy centre of eschatological fulfilment (I have dealt with this more fully in my book *Galiläa und Jerusalem*.)

They see in Jesus the Son of Man, still hidden but soon to reveal Himself; they consider themselves the poor and the elect; they wait patiently and humbly, in love and moderation, for the *Parousia* of the Lord and their own deliverance; they celebrate the Meal as an eschatological pledge; and with it they rejoice in their freedom from Jewish cult and sacrifice. We have now seen that this attitude is a true inheritance from their Lord and Master, and that it repeats on a smaller scale that freedom and restrictedness which was and is the sign of the hidden work and fulfilment of the Son of Man. To crown this inheritance a great and historically new thing has arisen: the Meal of the original "Galilean" community, a daily meal, a love-feast, and an eschatological celebration of the presence of the Lord and the corporateness of the "brethren," which remains for all its three aspects essentially one—the Lord's Meal, the Lord's Supper. It marks the beginning of a new Christian cult, which in virtue of its eschatological holiness overthrows all previous cults, and the beginning of a new community which is in the eschatological sense the community of the holy ones.

PRINTED IN GREAT BRITAIN BY
OLIVER AND BOYD LTD.
EDINBURGH

ERNST LOHMEYER confines his investigation of the relation of cult and gospel to the period of Jesus' own ministry and the early Church's transmission of his teachings. He begins with a well-known phenomenon : within a century after Jesus' time temples were desolate and sacrifices had been abandoned.

Probing for answers, Lohmeyer notes that Jesus says " No " to everything that is Jewish cult and at the same time " Yes " to preserving the traditional elements that lie within it. From this enigma the Christian cult came into being, displaying itself first and foremost in Baptism and Lord's Supper.

One thing alone explains the passing of all ancient cult and the emergence of Christian cult, says Lohmeyer—the original content and the original self-sufficient power of the Gospel itself. This poses another problem : Where in the Gospel tradition do we find any words which could be taken to indicate the birth of a new cult ?

Having posed the problems, Lohmeyer searches the Gospels for clues on the nature of Christian cult. Finally he discusses the eschatological aspects of this new cult and its interaction with the Gospel.